The Library Treasures of
St John's College, Cambridge

2018

A gift to Daddy from
the Master, Prof. Chris Dobson
on the occasion of his 100th
Birthday celebrations, including
Lunch in College with Jilly &
David.
Passed with love to Christopher,
January. 2022. from Jilly
xx

The Library Treasures of
St John's College, Cambridge

edited by Mark Nicholls and Kathryn McKee

Supported by
The National Lottery®
through the Heritage Lottery Fund

heritage
lottery fund

THIRD MILLENNIUM
PUBLISHING, LONDON

Contents

KEY: ■ Medieval manuscript ■ Post-medieval manuscript ■ Archives ■ Printed book ■ Artefact ■ Personal papers ■ Map

Contributors

Ruth Abbott, University Lecturer in the Long Nineteenth Century, Faculty of English, University of Cambridge, and Fellow of Lucy Cavendish College

Richard Beadle, Professor, Faculty of English, University of Cambridge, and Fellow of St John's College

Jesse D. Billett, Assistant Professor, Trinity College, University of Toronto. Formerly Fellow of St John's College

Katherine Birkwood, Rare Books and Special Collections Librarian, Royal College of Physicians. Former Hoyle Project Associate, St John's College Library

James P. Carley, Distinguished Research Professor Emeritus, York University, Toronto, and Professor of the History of the Book, University of Kent

Adam Crothers, Library Assistant, St John's College, and independent scholar

Graham Davies, Emeritus Professor of Old Testament Studies, University of Cambridge and Fellow of Fitzwilliam College

Christopher de Hamel, Donnelley Fellow Librarian, Corpus Christi College, Cambridge

Jeevan Deol, Affiliated Research Associate, Faculty of Asian and Middle Eastern Studies, University of Cambridge. Formerly Fellow of St John's College

Robin Glasscock, former University Lecturer, Department of Geography, University of Cambridge and Fellow of St John's College

Peter Goddard, Professor, School of Natural Sciences, Institute for Advanced Study, Princeton, New Jersey. Fellow and formerly Master of St John's College

Roger Hellyer, independent scholar

Boyd Hilton, Professor, Faculty of History, University of Cambridge, and Fellow of Trinity College

Ian McKee, writer and historian

Kathryn McKee, Sub-Librarian, St John's College

Simon Mitton, Fellow of St Edmund's College, Cambridge

Máire Ní Mhaonaigh, University Reader in Celtic, University of Cambridge and Fellow of St John's College

Mark Nicholls, Librarian, St John's College

Stella Panayotova, Keeper of Manuscripts and Printed Books, Fitzwilliam Museum, University of Cambridge

Michael Reeve, Emeritus Kennedy Professor of Latin, University of Cambridge, and Fellow of Pembroke College

Richard Rex, Reader in Reformation History, University of Cambridge, and Fellow of Queens' College

Malcolm Underwood, formerly Archivist, St John's College

Hugo Vickers, writer and broadcaster

Rebecca Watts, Butler Project Associate, St John's College Library, 2011–13

Opposite: Title page from John Fisher, Assertionis Lutheranae confutatio (1523).

οὐαι προφηταισ παραφροῦσιν ἐπομένοισ τῷ πνεύματι αυτῦ καὶ ουδὲν ὁρῶσι.

ASSERTIONIS
LVTHERANAE CONFVTATIO
Per Reuerendum Patrem Ioannem Roffensem
Episcopum, Academiæ Cantabrigiensis
Cancellarium.

CVM PRIVILE.	PRIVILEGIVM
gio Imperiali	Sereniss. Regis An.
in triennium.	gliæ reperies in
	proxima pagina

APVD INCLYTAM ANTVER=
piam in ædibus Honesti viri Michaelis Hil=
lenij. An. M. D. XXIII. postridie
Calen. Ianuar.

Edmundus Tyndall

Væ ⁊pphetis insipientibus, qui sequunt spiritū suū, & nihil vidēt, Ezechie.13.

אֲחַר רוּחָם וּלְבִלְהִי רָאוּ

What Makes the Library Special?

My introduction to the University of Cambridge occurred when I learned that my doctoral advisor was a Cambridge man. Although my dissertation dealt with general relativity, my real interest was geometry. Consequently, I spent the Lent, Easter and summer of 1968 studying geometry with Sir William Hodge. This work was so fruitful that I returned to Cambridge for the summers of 1969 and 1970.

In 2000, I was working on a scientific biography of the polymath Harry Bateman (1882–1946) at the California Institute of Technology. One of his tutors, actually a distant relative, was a Fellow of St John's College. I wrote to the Archivist at St John's and he replied that if I could come to Cambridge someone would be available to assist me. As soon as my spring classes ended I returned to Cambridge and met Jonathan Harrison, then the Special Collections Librarian at St John's College. He was very eager and enthusiastic about locating the extant Bateman material. Previously, I had used the archival material at the University of California at Los Angeles, Caltech and Library of Congress Manuscript

Division in Washington, DC, but Jonathan's assistance was unique. It would be fair to say that if I asked for one item, he would find three related items. When he left St John's several years ago, Mrs Kathryn McKee replaced him. While I have not met her personally, she has been extremely helpful.

I believe that somewhere I saw a phrase 'Investors in People' at St John's. These are not hollow words; St John's College Library has a magnificent collection of manuscripts, books and prints. Even better, the Library staff are eager to help people and find the material they need, whether

or not they have any connection with the College. In my experience this is simply remarkable!

Since my last visit in 2001, I have been very pleased to make annual donations to St John's College via Cambridge in America, in New York City. These donations have always been specified for the College Library. The Librarian Dr Mark Nicholls has been very helpful, and during the last two years I have suggested that some part of my donation be used for this most welcome book describing some particular treasures of the Library.

Professor Joseph D. Zund, New Mexico State University

Introduction

St John's College Library is as old as St John's College. The statutes approved in 1524 by John Fisher, Bishop of Rochester and Chancellor of the University, insisted that the College should 'possess and preserve a Library', and St John's has scrupulously honoured these obligations ever since. In the sixteenth century the Library was necessarily in the only Court then built, occupying rooms on the first floor to the south of the Great Gate overlooking St John's Street. Even by the standards of the day the collection held there was small: an inventory of 1558 recorded only seventy volumes. Such books as there were stood chained on the shelves, after the medieval fashion.

At the close of the sixteenth century, fashions began to change. Institutional libraries grew in size and St John's found itself confronting the possibility of large donations of scholarly books for which no shelf-space was available. The building now known as the Old Library was erected in the 1620s thanks to a donation from John Williams, Bishop of Lincoln and Lord Keeper of the Great Seal. His initials ILCS (Iohannes Lincolniensis Custos Sigilli) are found with the date 1624 – the year in which the roof went on – over the magnificent west-facing oriel window. Williams' library continues the northern range of Second Court down to the River Cam, with the first-floor library built over accommodation for Fellows and students, as the Bishop specifically requested.

Given the date, it is no surprise to find locally sourced materials and fittings after the Jacobean style. The local carpenter, Henry Mann, constructed the lovely bookcases. Bricks were purchased in Northampton and the floor was laid in the spring of 1625, timber being brought by river, the most practical method of bulk delivery to Cambridge in the days before railways and smooth roads. Details of the construction work come readily to hand: specific records of expenditure survive in the College Archives. When the doors eventually opened in 1628, the enjoyable task of filling the new shelves began.

Until recent times, Colleges have relied on bequests and donations to develop their library collections. The seventeenth century witnessed gifts which rank today among the most munificent ever received by St John's: volumes from the library of the Church of England preacher William Crashaw, from the collection of Charles I's Attorney General, Sir Robert Heath, from Francis Dee, Bishop of Peterborough, and Thomas Morton, Bishop of Durham, and from the long-serving Master of the College Humphrey Gower, alongside gifts large and

small from so many other Johnians, are among the thousands of items received during these years. Crashaw's library, presented via another member of the College, William Shakespeare's one-time patron the third Earl of Southampton, and his son the fourth Earl, is particularly strong in early manuscripts. As the proud home of what was then the largest library in Cambridge, St John's welcomed as visitors distinguished guests from across Europe, displaying through its collections the learning and scholarship to be found within the university. Charles I, Charles II, Samuel Pepys and John Evelyn were among those who strolled down the Upper Library, 130 feet (forty metres) from door to oriel window. Evelyn at least liked what he saw. After his visit in 1654 he described the Library – correctly – as the 'fairest in that university'.

Above: The Upper Library today, looking east. Right inset: A copy of John Fisher's Assertionis Lutheranae confutatio *(1523), bound in Cambridge by Garrett Godfrey. Opposite: Portrait of John Williams, Bishop of Lincoln, by Gilbert Jackson.*

Most libraries fill up eventually, the impulse to plug gaps trumping the tedious, sometimes agonising chore of removing obsolete texts. But Williams' generosity had allowed the College to accommodate growth over the long term, and pressure on space did not become acute until the eighteenth century. A long-time Fellow of the College, the Durham-born antiquarian Thomas Baker, was in 1717 thrown out of his Fellowship as a 'non juror' – someone, that is, who refused to swear allegiance to the first Hanoverian king, George I. While taking the new oath themselves, other Fellows were, however, quietly sympathetic, and permitted Baker to remain resident in College. Thereafter he inscribed his books with both his name and the words 'socius ejectus' – ejected Fellow – perhaps a mark of pride in his unique status, or perhaps an expression of ongoing irritation. At his death, in 1740, the Library received some 800 volumes from his impressive collection, additions to the 400 or so books that Baker presented in his lifetime. Rather than throw out older works to make room for these newcomers, the College accommodated Baker's donation by raising almost all the 'middle' cases in the Library, while preserving their now impractical but still decorative lectern tops.

In St John's the pace of things, donations included, slackened during the eighteenth century, but by the 1850s, spurred on by cheaper editions, university reforms, scholarly advances, evangelical zeal and a Victorian work ethic, the Library collections were once again expanding. Now, for the first time, they encroached on the

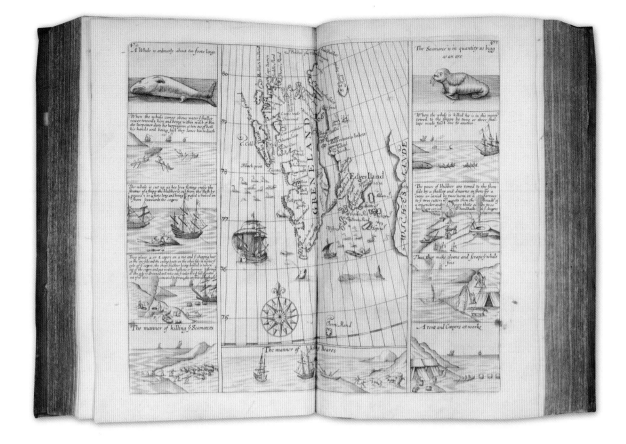

ground floor. The so-called Lower Library has ever since been linked to what is known today as the Upper Library by a spiral staircase – elegant, but not always easy to use when carrying large volumes. Colleges run on precedent and the first bookcases in the Lower Library were designed to match the shelving upstairs. But precedent was in this case soon abandoned, both because of cost and also because adjustable shelving – unheard of in the seventeenth century – proved more practical.

This book selects and describes some very special items held today in both Upper and Lower Libraries, and also includes a number of documents on the shelves of the extensive institutional Archive, now housed in a new home within the College's oldest building, the thirteenth-century School of Pythagoras, in the grounds west of the River Cam. Selection has been difficult, for a glance at relevant catalogues will confirm that the Old Library – 'Designated' of national and international importance under the Museums, Libraries and Archives Council's Designation scheme, now administered by the Arts Council – is home to many treasures, ranging widely in subject and in time. In

the Reading Room of the Old Library readers may examine, using fully modernised facilities, their own choices from the 33,000 books in the Upper Library, most of which date from before 1800. Indeed, 340 of these books are incunables – works printed before 1500. The earliest printed book in the Library is a 1466 edition of Cicero's *De officiis*, printed in Mainz, while the earliest book in the collection printed in Britain is a 1481 translation of Cicero's *De senectute*, from William Caxton's London printing press. One of the two Library copies of Caxton's *De senectute*, which formerly belonged to the English Civil War general Sir Thomas Fairfax, arrived in the Library as part of a fine collection of incunables bequeathed to St John's by one of its eighteenth-century Masters, John Newcome. The Library has Newcome to thank, too, for its beautiful 1474 edition of Ovid's works formerly owned by members of the illustrious, and notorious, Medici family, rulers of the city state of Florence.

Many volumes on the shelves of the Upper Library demonstrate equally fascinating provenances. Former owners include Elizabeth I's long-serving Secretary and Treasurer Lord Burghley and the Elizabethan astrologer, scientist and

Among more than 270 medieval manuscripts in the St John's collection are a tenth-century psalter (the biblical Psalms) from an Irish monastery, a thirteenth-century psalter with a series of more than forty full-page illuminations showing familiar episodes from the Old and New Testaments and related traditions, an early version of Geoffrey Chaucer's *Troilus and Criseyde,* and a fifteenth-century Book of Hours, or devotional manual, containing an inscription in the handwriting of Lady Margaret Beaufort, mother of Henry VII and Foundress of St John's College, seeking prayers from her lady-in-waiting. Lady Margaret's inscription faces an illuminated depiction of St John at work on his Gospel, and many consider that the juxtapositions of learning and prayer, of Foundress and Patron Saint, sum up the enduring aims of the College. These manuscripts are described

proponent of imperial expansion John Dee, both Johnians, and that far less illustrious alumnus Titus Oates, contriver of the Popish Plot hysteria during the reign of Charles II. John Collins, Professor of Physic, left a fine collection of sixteenth-century medical works at his death in 1634. Matthew Prior – poet, diplomat and spy – bequeathed around 300 works, relating for the most part to French literature and history, while Charles Otway, a Fellow who died in 1721, accumulated and presented thousands of English sermons and political pamphlets. Predictably, in an academic community, the College holds first editions of the most influential scholarly books, for example Isaac Newton's *Principia* and Charles Darwin's *Origin of Species*, the latter an inscribed copy annotated by the Johnian polymath Samuel Butler, a one-time friend of Darwin who did not share his views on evolution.

....

Above: Portrait of John Newcome by an unidentified artist. **Right:** *Portrait of Lady Margaret Beaufort by Rowland Lockey.* **Opposite:** Purchas his pilgrimes *(1625) illustration from volume 3.*

*Left: Portrait of Henry Wriothesley, third Earl of Southampton, after Michiel Jan van Miereld. **Below:** Victor Hugo notebook, MS N.30.*

Edward Henry Palmer's travels in nineteenth-century Palestine and Egypt, and notebooks compiled by Victor Hugo, presented by the widow of Professor Jean-Bertrand Barrère, a Fellow of the College.

Elsewhere in the Old Library there are wonderful collections of personal papers, reflecting in particular the work of Johnian scientists. Holdings include papers of John Couch Adams, the co-discoverer of the planet Neptune, of the eminent geophysicist Sir Harold Jeffreys, of Sir Maurice Wilkes, who oversaw the building of the first programmable computer in the UK, and of Sir Fred Hoyle, renowned for his work on the formation of elements within stars, the man who coined the term 'big bang'. The arts and humanities are represented too, in the papers, photographs, music and paintings of Samuel Butler, the diaries of the archaeologist and TV personality Glyn Daniel, and the correspondence and diaries of the society photographer and Oscar-winning designer Sir Cecil Beaton. The papers of the author Lyn Newman (née Lyn Irvine) include extensive correspondence from the 1920s and 1930s with members of the Bloomsbury

further in the following pages. Later manuscripts include the earliest surviving version of Sir Philip Sidney's *Arcadia*, papers relating to the execution of Mary, Queen of Scots, secret correspondence touching on arrangements for the Restoration of Charles II, records relating to Professor

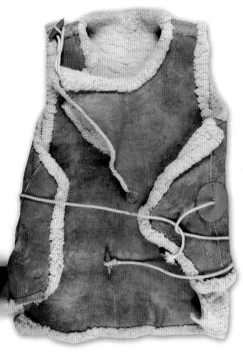

Group and their friends, among them Leonard Woolf and E. M. Forster, as well as with the philosopher Bertrand Russell. The Library also holds papers of the best-selling Johnian author Douglas Adams. Members of St John's College have in their time helped shape the modern world, as cabinet ministers, as civil servants and through principled activism: the Library holds papers of the anti-slavery campaigners Thomas Clarkson and William Wilberforce. Letters written by Lord Burghley are found alongside those of Viscount Castlereagh, one of the most prominent statesmen of the nineteenth century. There is also a collection of letters relating to Lord Palmerston, Prime Minister in the 1850s and 1860s.

The Library catalogue ranges far beyond materials associated with the 'great and good'. The undergraduate Alan Hiller served and died on the Western Front during the First World War and his letters provide a poignant insight into life in the trenches. Closer to home, Stephen Notcutt, a future solicitor in Ipswich, provides a glimpse of events at St John's in the 1880s through a fine sequence of undergraduate letters to his mother. The correspondence of Ernest Benians, Master of St John's from 1933 to 1952, also illustrates his years as a student in the College, while the diaries of T. R. Glover, Fellow, Classical scholar and University Orator, enlighten us on College personalities and politics early in the twentieth century. A lively journal of student life in the 1840s and the poetry of Hugh Sykes Davies demonstrate the diversity of papers held in the Library.

Cambridge college libraries are sometimes likened to museums, and it is true that the collections held there range far beyond the printed book and the written archive. The photographs of everyday life at St John's from the 1870s onwards; the materia medica cabinet of William Heberden, eighteenth-century 'father of rheumatology', complete with a

*Above: Fleece worn by Vice Admiral Sir Bruce Fraser the night the Scharnhorst was sunk in 1943. From the Hoyle Collection. **Right:** Portrait of William Heberden by Sir William Beechey.*

mummified lizard and an equally desiccated mushroom, two centuries old and half a metre across; the physicist Paul Dirac's Nobel Prize medal and certificate; a Tudor comb; something best described as a 'lead skull'; College rugby blazers from the nineteenth century; a fleece worn by the Admiral of the British fleet that sank the German battleship *Scharnhorst* in the winter darkness of the Arctic Ocean on Boxing Day 1943; and a life mask of William Wordsworth, taken by the artist Benjamin Haydon, are just a few among so many evocative artefacts.

The College's collections of Greek and Roman coins are on loan to the Fitzwilliam Museum in Cambridge, while astronomical instruments once used in the College's observatory – dismantled in the mid-nineteenth century when light pollution made town-centre observational astronomy all but impossible – are held under similar arrangements by the University's Whipple Museum of the History of Science. Readers will nevertheless find in these pages a description of one treasure from the old observatory still to be seen in St John's: an exceptional long-case chronometer made by John Shelton stands in the Library's Exhibition Area, which is open to the public on weekdays through most of the year.

The public are particularly welcome, and there is always something interesting to see in this Exhibition Area. Over the past two decades Library and Archives staff have curated many displays on subjects as diverse as College rooms, St John's in wartime, Johnian science fiction, 'all-conquering Death' and College sport. Information on forthcoming exhibitions is available on the Library website.

The Working Library

While the scope of this book is specific, St John's College Library is much more than a historical treasure house. It offers a vital service to our current Fellows, undergraduates and graduate students, and does so more effectively than at any other time in the history of the College. The modern student works in a new Library, designed by the architect Edward Cullinan and sharing the same front door with the Old Library Building. Cullinan's 'Working Library' holds core works – and much else besides – for every subject now taught in the University. Readers come and go at any time of the day or night, enjoying access to a collection of more than 100,000 textbooks, reference works and journals, all housed in comfortable surroundings. Borrowing is available at all hours thanks to an automated system, while unobtrusive security arrangements guard both building and stock. Every desk either has its own PC facilities or offers connectivity to the Internet, allowing readers to choose from a vast range of electronic journals, e-books and other online resources provided to resident members of the University. Light and airy study spaces, designated quiet areas, a large, well-equipped meeting room, a diverse audio-visual collection, refreshment facilities and some of the best Library views in Cambridge all enhance the learning experience.

Mark Nicholls and Kathryn McKee

Above: A comfortable base for readers, the new Working Library.

Editorial Note

Bibliographic citations and references have been limited to essential details. Further particulars are readily available on the College Library's website (www.joh.cam.ac.uk/library). The original spelling of most quotations has been retained, but some modernisation of punctuation has been attempted for the sake of clarity.

Besides acknowledging our debt to the various contributors, which is great, and to Carl Impey for his wonderful photographs, we are most grateful to the following for their invaluable assistance in producing this book. Joel Burden, Bonnie Murray, Neil Titman and Susan Pugsley of Third Millennium have always been on hand with encouragement and expert guidance. Our colleagues in the College Library have discussed interesting points and contributed in many other ways; we would draw particular attention to the parts played by Adam Crothers, who was recruited to the list of contributors late in the day, and Charlotte Hoare, who read and commented on the text. Ryan Cronin in the College's Communications Office and Jill Slater in the Finance Office have also facilitated our work at more than one problematic juncture. The Archivist, Tracy Wilkinson, has overseen the conservation and production of those items that fall within her charge. Jonathan Harrison, formerly Special Collections Librarian, was closely involved in the initial selection of treasures, as was the former Archivist – and contributor to this volume – Malcolm Underwood. Essential conservation work to facilitate description and photography was carried out at various times by George Bolton, and by Edward Cheese and his colleagues at the Cambridge Colleges' Conservation Consortium, drawing in part on a grant from the National Manuscripts Conservation Trust. The Heritage Lottery Fund gave most generous support across five years to cataloguing and outreach projects on the collections of Samuel Butler and Fred Hoyle, and the American Institute of Physics also supported work on the Hoyle Collection that has contributed to the description that follows in these pages. Our greatest debt is of course to Professor Joseph Zund. Without his constant encouragement, shown in so many ways, this volume would never have seen the light of day.

For permission to reproduce photographs we thank the Master and Fellows of St John's College, Paul Everest (pp. 8–9, 16), Michael Noakes PPROI RP (p. 146) and Brian A. Jackson (pp. 122, 123).

Prized for a Thousand Years

The Psalms of David, late tenth century. St John's College MS C.9

The so-called Southampton Psalter is a beautifully executed illuminated Irish psalm book dating to around the turn of the first millennium. It was among a group of books donated to St John's College in 1635 by Thomas Wriothesley, Earl of Southampton. Thomas's father, Henry, William Shakespeare's patron, had acquired the books from the bibliophile William Crashaw (d. 1626), also a former member of the College. It was through this connection that the Psalter acquired the name by which it is now known.

This wonderful book had been in England for some considerable time before it was acquired by St John's: it is known to have formed part of the collection of the Priory of St Martin at Dover in 1389, as it is included in a catalogue of these volumes made by John Whytefield in that year. Moreover, corrections made to the manuscript in the twelfth century are in an English hand. Its Irish origin is indicated by the nature of its script and decoration. In addition, the specific text of the psalms employed (the *Gallicanum* version) and the precise ordering of the material are typical of other Irish psalters of the period. Most notably, the manuscript is annotated, or glossed, in medieval Irish as well as Latin, and while much of this glossed material was copied from an earlier source, a short contemporary phrase in the vernacular, 'Mayday today, namely on Wednesday' (*Beltene inndiu .i. for cetain*), provides a vivid glimpse of a scribe at his task.

That scribe was one of four or five individuals engaged in writing the manuscript, though we can discern one main scribe who used a variety of scripts (Insular half-uncial and Insular minuscule) to indicate the relative importance of different types of text, from the Scriptures with their lesser significant headings (*tituli*) down to explanatory material pertaining to the psalms. Thus this was a planned, unified book concerned with the visual, though it may have been influenced by the layout of the exemplar upon which it drew. Its appeal to the eye is underlined by its striking illuminations, three of which occupy full pages, marking in turn the beginning of a set of fifty psalms. These figure illustrations – of David fighting the lion, the Crucifixion, and David and Goliath – are similarly designed with central unity in mind. In the same way, the pattern of large decorated initials marking the beginning of each of the one hundred and fifty psalms, supplemented by the occurrence of smaller coloured initials at regular intervals, is also indicative of a carefully conceived work.

The Southampton Psalter was always a precious book. It was used for scholarly purposes and well-known earlier commentaries supply much of the explicatory text surrounding the psalms. Interpretative modes characteristic of other psalters of the period are attested therein, including the allegorical focusing on figurative meaning, and to a lesser extent the historical favouring a more literal understanding of the words. More than one approach is often applied to the same psalm, resulting in a work of advanced learning. It is therefore fitting that St John's College should have become its home.

Máire Ní Mhaonaigh

....

Opposite: The Crucifixion, fo. 35v.

An Elevated Form of Music

Triple Psalter, Rheims, early twelfth century. St John's College MS B.18

This twelfth-century manuscript is a 'triple psalter', containing three Latin translations of the psalms in parallel columns: the Vulgate of St Jerome; the so-called *Psalterium Romanum*; and Jerome's *Psalterium iuxta Hebraeos*, translated directly from the original Hebrew. Several leaves of introductory matter, by Jerome and other authors, are provided to prepare the reader for careful study of the biblical text. The psalms are followed by a set of liturgical texts (canticles, creeds and a litany of the saints), and the decoration of the manuscript follows a liturgical pattern. Elaborate initials mark the first psalm sung at Matins and Vespers on each day of the week, according to the liturgical use of a cathedral or parish church as opposed to a Benedictine monastery.

There are two full-page illustrations. The first is a celebrated depiction of two kinds of music. In an upper panel King David plucks a lyre, while attendants play musical instruments capable of the 'rational sound' (*vox articulata*) of the octave scale: seven bells, an organ with two ranks of seven pipes, and a pan-flute and a cornett, each with seven holes. The bell-ringer tunes a monochord in the 1:2 ratio of the perfect octave. Significantly, a singer holds a copy of the Book of Psalms. In the lower panel, the central figure is a bear thumping a drum, flanked by dancers and tumblers who frolic to the 'animalistic sound' (*vox confusa*) of a hunter's horn and a fiddle. Chanting the psalms is thus classed as a rational, elevated form of music.

In the second full-page illustration, an upper panel shows Christ crucified on a tree-like cross whose base is continuous with a leafy tree in the lower panel, where an angel seated on the empty tomb announces the Resurrection to the three women, as in the Gospels. The image directly precedes the first psalm, and medieval commentators read Psalm 1:3 as a veiled reference to the Cross and Resurrection of Christ: 'he shall be like a tree planted by the rivers of water'.

The selection of saints in the litany, together with its petition for 'the people of St Mary and St Remigius', strongly suggests that the psalter was made for the cathedral church of Notre-Dame in Rheims, and it has been shown that the psalms and introductory texts were copied from an eleventh-century psalter owned by the Rheims cathedral chapter. The litany, however, mentions two English martyrs, Alban and Edmund, and the distinguished liturgist F. E. Warren thought the wording of two of the litany's petitions indicated an English origin – perhaps one of the English monasteries listed in Domesday Book as possessions of the Abbey of Saint-Remi in Rheims. But the same two petitions are found in a litany in a ninth-century Rheims psalter (Cambridge, Corpus Christi College MS 272, folio 154r), and, as has already been mentioned, the manuscript's decoration implies a cathedral, not a monastic liturgy. The litany itself mentions 'our archbishop' but not 'our abbot'. English saints are not unknown in French litanies, and one transcribed by the medievalist Jean Mabillon (1632–1707) from a tenth-century manuscript in the Rheims Cathedral library, now lost, included a petition 'for the clergy and people of England'. So there is little reason to doubt that the manuscript was copied at Rheims.

Jesse D. Billett

....

Opposite: Juxtaposition of sacred and profane music, fo. 1r.

Rebel against Rome

Flavius Josephus, *History of the Jewish War*, early twelfth century. St John's College MS A.8

Titus Flavius Josephus, or, to give him his earlier name, Joseph ben Matityahu, was the author of particularly important written sources for the history and antiquities of the Holy Land in the first century after the birth of Christ. The leader of a rebel force during the Jewish revolt against Rome in the late 60s AD, Josephus was captured by the Romans, changed sides, and was present at the siege of Jerusalem in AD 70, witnessing the destruction and looting of the city. Josephus's parents and wife died in the siege. His *History of the Jewish War* is thus both an objective record for a Roman audience and also, in part, a justification of his own ambiguous role in a bloody conflict.

This handsome volume dates from the first half of the twelfth century. It is the second of two volumes undertaken by monks at Christ Church Priory, Canterbury, one of the best-known and finest monastic 'scriptoria' (places where books were copied) in England at that time. Although it fell into different hands when the Library was dispersed in the sixteenth century, the companion volume is today also in Cambridge, among the wonderful medieval collections of the University Library. MS A.8 contains the latter sections of Josephus's later work, the *Antiquities of the Jews*, a source of great importance for those interested in life in Roman Judea around the time of Jesus's ministry. The full text of the *History of the Jewish War* follows on, beginning with a particularly handsome hand-coloured initial 'C', showing a monk named Samuel figuratively copying from the original supported by Josephus himself. Samuel holds both quill and the essential sharpening knife required for precise penmanship. Since no 'Samuel' has been identified in connection with Josephus, it is tempting to identify him with the scribe working in Canterbury nearly nine centuries ago – which makes this little figure an early self-portrait.

The manuscript formed one part of the greatest donation of early texts ever received by St John's, that presented by Thomas, fourth Earl of Southampton, in the 1630s. Southampton acquired the books from his father, Henry Wriothesley, the third Earl and Shakespeare's one-time patron, who had in turn received them from the antiquary and religious controversialist William Crashaw, author of *Romish Forgeries and Falsifications* (1606). The manuscript was old then. It is worth reflecting that this lovely book takes us almost halfway back in time to the momentous and controversial events described by Josephus.

Mark Nicholls

Opposite: A scribe, Samuel, copies from a text held by Josephus, fo. 103v.

EXPLICIT PROLOGVS·

INCIPIT LIBER PRIMVS HYSTORIARVM IOSEPH DE BELLO IVDAIC·

VM POTENTES IVDEORV
INTERSE
DISSIDE
RENT EO
TEMPORE
QUO detota

...cei ad antiochum confugerunt
tentes ut semet ducib; inuideam
petit. Idq; regi psuasum est. ia
sic animato. Quare cum magnis
tum copijs egressus ex ciuitate for
expugnatam capit. & maxima e
multitudine quib; ptholomeus
or erat interfect. elataq; passim
ltatib; predandi licentia ipse ex
expoliauit. & cotidiane religionis
duitatem pannos tres sexq; menses
hibuit. Pontifex autem onias eff
ad ptholomeu. acceptoq; ab eo
liopolitana regione solo ibi o
pidum condidit ierosolimis simi
templumq; edificauit. De quib;
opportune referemus. Verumtamen
antiocho neq; preter spem deuict
tas neq; populatio nec tanta edefi
fuerunt. sed intemperantia uiror
memoria que inobsidione pate
iudeos cogere cepit ut abrogar
re patrio nec infantes suos circum
rent. portosq; sup aram immola
quib; omis aduersabantur. optim
quisq; ppterea trucidabatur. Et tam
des presidiis ab antiocho preposit
ad naturalem crudelitatem sui p
ptis impijs obsecundans. omnem
iniquitatis excessit. cum hic singul
uiros honorabiles uerberauit. ea
inter cotidie speciem capta urbis

A Scholar's Dream Come True

An anthology of spiritual wisdom, England, probably Worcester, *c.* 1140.
St John's College MS B.20

I n twelfth-century England, this volume would have been a dream come true for any preacher with passion for learning and beauty. Vignettes and initials in a rich palette of gold and other colours adorn the fascinating compilation of computistical, theological and homiletic texts.

The manuscript opens with tables of the lunar cycle that facilitated the calculation of the date of Easter. These are followed by a Calendar, which includes the feast days of two bishops of Worcester, St Ecgwine (d. *c.* 717) and St Oswald (d. 992), both penned by the original scribe. A third bishop, Wulfstan II (d. 1095), was added in a thirteenth-century hand, presumably after his canonisation in 1203. While the manuscript may not have been made at or for Worcester Cathedral Priory, it was probably intended for use within the diocese or for presentation to an external recipient interested in Worcester traditions. Next come Easter tables which cover the period 1140–1504 and indicate that the manuscript was made in or about the year 1140.

The longest units represent two collections of sermons. The first originated on the Continent and had reached England by the middle of the tenth century. The second is a blend of old and new. Some of its texts, notably St Wulfstan's homilies, or instructional religious discourses, point to Worcester sources, while sermons by Geoffrey of Loroux, Archbishop of Bordeaux (d. 1158), show a concerted effort to supplement the patristic, Carolingian and Anglo-Saxon material with up-to-date texts. The *Liber de differentiis rerum* ('Book on the difference of things') by Isidore, Archbishop of Seville (d. 636), explains central Christian doctrines, such as the Trinity and the two natures of Christ. The *Liber scintillarum*

('Book of sparks') by Defensor, a monk at Ligugé near Poitiers (d. *c.* 717), contains over 2500 sayings from the Bible and the Church Fathers. Isidore and Defensor's texts were popular works, often excerpted by authors of sermons.

The manuscript was made by a competent team of at least four scribes and two artists. Two members of this team stand out: the artist of the Calendar scenes and the opening initial of Isidore's text, and the scribe who penned the elegant script at the beginning and the end of the volume. A date in the 1140s seems consistent with both script and decoration, which find parallels in manuscripts associated with Worcester, Hereford and Gloucester from *c.* 1130 to *c.* 1150. Particularly indicative are the architectural frame of the Nativity scene at folio 4r, the exuberant blossoms with their central 'tongues' wrapped round the foliage coils (folio 6r), and the folds of the drapery arranged in clusters of nested Vs in the Calendar scenes at folio 2v. The Anglo-Saxon technique of multi-colour drawing survived into the second quarter of the twelfth century, notably at Worcester, where St Wulfstan's long episcopate ensured the continuation of Anglo-Saxon traditions and their gradual integration with Norman features. The latter include the multi-coloured backgrounds, the emphatically enlarged hands, and the initial formed of dragons and a lion-head human figure at folio 6r. Exquisite arabesque initials mark text divisions throughout the volume, displaying the fluid energy and organic vitality of English Romanesque art.

Stella Panayotova

....

Opposite: Calendar and signs of the Zodiac, fo. 2v. **Insert:** *A detail from fo. 6r.*

A Revolutionary Bible

The New Testament, late twelfth century. St John's College MS G.15

The mid-twelfth century represents a very interesting moment in the history of the Bible. Before then, the Scriptures were known in Europe either in their separate and individual components, such as the Pentateuch or the Gospels, or else – and generally only from the late eleventh century – as huge sets of gigantic volumes so big that it can take several people to move them. They were monumental manuscripts for public use. The Bible as we know it today, as a single portable volume for private study, containing the entire corpus of texts from Genesis to Revelation in tiny script, was invented around 1150. It is generally assumed that this happened in Paris, probably to help the teaching needs of the schools of theology in the Augustinian Abbey of St-Victor.

The first monastery in England to seize upon these new developments was that of St Albans. The abbot there, Simon, who held office from 1167 to 1183, had corresponded with St-Victor about obtaining new texts. He clearly brought illuminators and scribes to England, probably from Paris. The *Gesta abbatum* of St Albans takes up the story: 'After he had been made abbot he continued to have fine books and volumes written of both the Old and New Testaments … faultlessly finished, which we have never seen bettered.' The monks were evidently astonished, calling them *authentica* – models of accuracy. The chronicler continues, 'Whoever wishes to see these books will find them in the painted cupboard in the church opposite the tomb of the holy Roger the hermit, where the abbot himself ordered them to be placed.'

MS G.15 is one of these very books. At the top of the first page is an inscription which begins, *Hunc libellum fecit dominus Symon abbas de sancti albani* ('Simon, abbot of St Albans, [had] this little book made'), followed by an anathema or curse against anyone who should ever steal it. Notice that word *libellum*, 'little book': this manuscript is minute. It is about 155mm by 105mm, hardly six by four inches, and it can easily be held in the palm of the hand. It has twenty-eight lines of tiny script within the height of about 103mm. Given our familiarity with small printed Bibles today, it is hard to realise what a revolutionary format this was in the second half of the twelfth century. It contains the entire New Testament, in the order of the Gospels, Acts, Canonical Epistles, Revelation and the Pauline Epistles, all compressed within two covers.

Abbot Simon also commissioned an entire portable Bible, now Cambridge, Corpus Christi College MS 48, with illumination which is in part copied from the St John's manuscript, or vice versa, for it is not certain which came first. Then the monks of St Albans began exporting copies of these new Bibles. One, now in Dublin (Trinity College MS 51), sent out to West Dereham Abbey in Norfolk, is apparently by the same scribe as the New Testament at St John's. By about 1200, almost all Bibles in England were portable volumes.

Christopher de Hamel

Opposite: The Book of Revelation, initial verses, image greatly enlarged, fo. 155v.

·I·

pocalipsis ihu xpi quã dedit ill
palam face seruis suis q̃ oportet fieri
⁊ significauit mittens p anglm suũ
suo ioħi. qui testimoniũ pħibat̄ ūb
⁊ testimoniũ ihu e̅ queq; uidit.
qui legit ⁊ q̃ audit uerba ꝓpħie hui:
uar ea q̃ i nea scpta sunt. Temp° app

·II·

Ioħs septem ecclIis q̃ sunt in asia. Grā uob ⁊ pax ab eo qui
erat: ⁊ q̃ uentur° e̅: ⁊ a septem spiritab qui inconspectu thꝛ
eius st̅: ⁊ ab ihu e̅ q̃ est testis fidelis ꝓmogenitus mortuoꝛ ⁊ pn
regum terre. Qui dilexit nos ⁊ lauit nos a peccatis n̅ris in sang
suo. ⁊ fecit nos regnũ ⁊ sacerdotes d̅o ⁊ patri suo. Ipsi g̅la ⁊ impi
ꝛ isc̅la sclꝵ acn̅. Ecce uenit cũ nubib° ⁊ uidebit eum omnis oc
q̃ cũ pupugerunt: ⁊ plangent se sup eum omis tribꝛ terre. etiā
Ego sum a.⁊.w. pncipiũ ⁊ finis dicit d̅n̅s d̅s. qui e̅ ⁊ q̃ erat: ⁊ qui
tur est omp̅s. Ego ioħs fr̅ ur ⁊ socius in tribulatõne ⁊ regno ⁊ p

·III·

entia in ihu: fui in insula q̃ uocat̄ pathmos. ꝓp uerbum d̅i ⁊
moniũ ihu xpi. Fui in sp̅u in d̅nica die. ⁊ audiui p me uocē ma
tanq̃m tube dicentis. Q̊d uides scribe in libro. ⁊ mitte septem
q̃ sunt in asia. epheso. ⁊ smyrne. ⁊ pgamo. ⁊ tyatire. ⁊ sardis. ⁊ p

·IIII·

delfie ⁊ laodicie. Et ꝙuersus sum: ut uidem uocē que loq̄bat
mecũ. Et ꝙ uidi septē candelabra aurea. ⁊ in medio septem

The Long Prayerful Road to Heaven

The Mortuary Roll of Amphelisa of Lillechurch, early thirteenth century.
St John's College MS N.31

At thirty-seven feet (eleven metres) long, and an average of seven inches (180 millimetres) wide, the mortuary roll of Amphelisa of Lillechurch is an extraordinary manuscript. It consists of nineteen pieces of parchment, some written on on both sides, stitched together to form a continuous roll. It travelled hundreds of miles to gather the contributions of over 370 different scribes.

Mortuary rolls were monastic documents which maintained the same format for over 500 years. Their purpose was to inform other religious establishments of the death of the head of a house, and to seek their prayers for the soul of the departed. On the death of their head, a house would start a roll with an encyclical letter, to which certificates or *tituli* would be added by each house to which the announcement was carried. Each *titulus* gave the dedication and location of the recipient, the name of the departed, and a prayer for his or her soul. A roll was a convenient format for carrying on lengthy journeys, and could easily be extended by adding further pieces of parchment. The bearer of the roll, usually a layman, was paid by the originating house, and hospitality was sought from each institution he visited. Such journeys, typically on foot, could be very lengthy, sometimes crossing several countries.

The mortuary roll of Amphelisa is one of the oldest in England. The first known is that of Turgot of Durham (d. 1115), followed by the roll of Reginald of Bath (d. 1190). Documents in the College Archives suggest that Amphelisa died between 1208 and 1214. Her roll was carried to 378 religious houses, belonging to a variety of orders, male and female, located throughout virtually every English county, in Monmouthshire, and in southern Scotland.

Founded in 1148 to house the community led by Mary, daughter of King Stephen, by 1521 the Benedictine Priory of Lillechurch in Kent had declined and fallen into disrepute. John Fisher, Bishop of Rochester and executor of Lady Margaret Beaufort, mother of Henry VII, secured its suppression and the appropriation of its lands to her new educational foundation of St John's College. The priory's documents also came to the College, including the mortuary roll.

Few rolls survive in their entirety, though many were circulated. In an age where no one, however blameless his or her life, was exempt from Purgatory, the prayers of the living were vital in easing the passage of the soul of the departed to Heaven. News of a religious leader's death was carried far beyond their own order or locality, to draw upon a wider community of prayer for their soul. However, having obtained the promise of prayers the rolls themselves had served their purpose, and became a useful source of scrap parchment. Fragments are preserved in the bindings of other documents, sometimes re-used no more than a generation after a roll's creation. That Amphelisa's roll has survived intact for 800 years owes much to Lillechurch's decline and the local bishop's interest in augmenting the endowment of St John's College.

Kathryn McKee

....

Opposite and overleaf: Encyclical letter and tituli from the mortuary roll.

[...]niu[er]s[is] xp[ist]i fidelib[us] p[rese]ntem paginam inspectur[is] Humil[es] Ancillar[um] [Christ]i conuent[us] eccl[es]ie s[an]c[t]e [...]
de Lillechirch[e] Salutem in d[omi]no sempiturn[am]. Post imbres lacrimar[um] [et] fletuu[m] inundatione q[...] in
transitu k[arissi]me d[omi]ne [et] m[at]ris n[ost]re piissime Amphelise p[ri]orisse [...]dum[...] que uacante d[omi]no qui
[...]odecimo kal[endas] februar[ii] am[...] nulla[m] in hanc uita[m] reu[er]tu[n]s ingressa celo terre q[...] debitu[m] humani g[ene]ris
p[er]soluit: terra quod s[uu]m e[st] recipien[s] [et] sp[irit]u re[uerten]te ad d[omi]nu[m] q[ui] fecit illum. [et] p[er]q[...] eg[re]g[...] sollt[...]
p[ro]pria exple[n]tium quib[us] ti heu[...] occ[...] in s[...] erebus singulis b[...] i[n]t[er] p[...]num manu[m] m[...]em ad chalamu[m]
inuisita[n] u[est]re scripto de[...] cante[...] chalamitate qu[...] pat[...]. Subtrac[t]a e[ni]m c[...]a n[ost]re. cam s[...] comne[...] iur[...] hac qua
ambulam[us] su[n]t [et] c[...]mu[n] delig[u]t nob. Ha[n]c e[ni]m dilect[...] d[e]o [et] ho[m]i[n]ib[us] q[uo]d insigne [et] i[n] h[ij]s qui p[rese]nt[...] i[n] o[m]nib[us] se[...]
ipsa[m] nob honor[...] op[...] p[re]buit exemplu[m]. Requiescebat in ea s[...] ur. p[er] q[ue]m licebat delectari in d[omi]no. meditari s[ibi] us. orare
sec[...]. erat e[ni]m nob exemplo ei[us] oratio p[...]guior. lectio frequentio[r]. [et] affect[...] seruentio[r]. s[ed] sublata e[st] [et] ub[...] omnia su[n]t
dolem[us] [et] i[n] d[omi]no ditissimi dolem[us] nob ademptu[m] tam dulce solatiu[m]. ta[m] fidele auxiliu[m]. tam salutare asilu[m]. Dole[n]-
t[...] q[ue] dole[n]da e[st]: s[ed] q[ue] ablata. Credim[us] e[ni]m q[uod] mors ei[us] in c[on]sp[ec]tu d[omi]ni sit p[re]tiosa. q[uia] p[er]cellerunt [et] sole[...] d[es]olation[...] insignia.
tam e[n]i[m] quasi[...] taceo p[re]cellere e[st] qui uit[re] hui[us] spacia p[...]isse poss[it]. qui s[alt]e in minorib[us] [et] leuib[us] p[ec]c[at]is frequente[r] offendat.
un[...] i[n]utilitate uita[m] recem[us] haur[...] ut n[ost]re hu[manita]ti d[eb]itum s[...]eis p[...]ce n[ost]re b[e]n[e]ficia o[rati]onum u[est]rarum i[m]pendat[is]. Tene-
mur itaq[ue] carit[at]is u[inc]lo quo relig[ios]i [et] s[an]c[t]i mu[tu]o ligant[ur] in d[omi]no. p[ro] def[u]nc[t]is u[est]ris exorare ut a p[ecca]tis soluant[ur].
Subuen[n]ite ig[itur] fr[atr]es k[arissi]mi anime p[ri]orisse n[ost]re defuncte p[re]cib[us] o[m]nib[us] u[est]ris. ut o[mn]i labe p[ur]gata. int[re]t in gaudiu[m] d[omi]ni. su[m]-
scipie[n]s cum s[an]c[t]is [et] el[e]c[t]is dei refrigerii sedem. quietis. beatitudine. humili clama[n]te. P[re]sta[n]te d[omi]no n[ost]ro ih[s]u xp[ist]o. cui
est honor [et] g[lor]ia in secula s[e]c[u]l[or]um. Amen.

Titulus s[an]c[t]i Andree ap[osto]li v officii[s] eccl[es]ie. Multiplicat p[ro]uocatio. tu[m] contiguitate lo-
cor[um]. tu[m] uicinitate religionis. maxime autem experi[enti]a be[ne]ficior[um]. lacrimas
effundim[us] qui testes su[n]t ut art[...] augustin[...] i[n]timi doloris. ea p[ro]pter co[m]patien[tes] co[m]-
collegio u[est]ro k[arissi]me d[omi]ne [et] honorabiles. a[n]i[m]am p[ri]orisse u[est]re [et] more solito absoluim[us]
absoluim[us]. [et] nomen ei[us] no[m]i[n]ib[us] f[rat]ru[m] u[est]ror[um] a[d]scripsim[us]. [et] in co[m]mune be[ne]ficiu[m] eccl[es]ie
n[ost]re plenarie recepim[us]. P[re]t[er]ea quia du[as] t[ri]cennalia in hoc anno in eccl[es]ia n[ost]ra celebratur[i] tu[m]i
hor[um] p[ar]ticip[e]m eam co[n]stituim[us]. S[ed] [et] un[usquisq]ue sacerdos pro ea t[r]es missas celeb[ra]b[it]. v eliqui in-
fer[i]oris ordinis: exp[...]ent seruitu[m] psalmor[um] celebra[n]t[...] p[er]soluet. Et[iam] d[omi]n[a] Amphelise p[ri]orisse
de h[...] Lillechirch[e]. [et] a[n]i[m]e o[mn]i[um] fideliu[m] defunctor[um] p[er] m[isericordi]am dei req[ui]escant in pace. Amen.
O[rem]us[?] pro u[ob]is orat[e] pro n[ob]is.

Titulus eccl[es]ie s[an]c[t]i Augustini Cant[uarie]. A[n]i[m]a d[omi]ne Amphelise p[ri]orisse de Lillechirch[e]. [et] a[n]i[m]e
o[mn]iu[m] fideliu[m] defuncto[rum] p[er] m[isericordi]am dei requiescant in pace. Amen. Concedam[us] e[st] co[m]mune b[e]n[e]fi-
ciu[m] eccl[es]ie n[ost]re. Orauim[us] p[ro] u[ob]is: orate pro nob[is].

Titulus eccl[es]ie s[an]c[t]i Gregorii Cant[uarie]. A[n]i[m]a d[omi]ne Amphelise p[ri]orisse de Lillech-
[ir]ch[e] [et] a[n]i[m]e o[mn]iu[m] fideliu[m] defuncto[rum] p[er] m[isericordi]am dei requiescant in pace. Am[en]
[...]

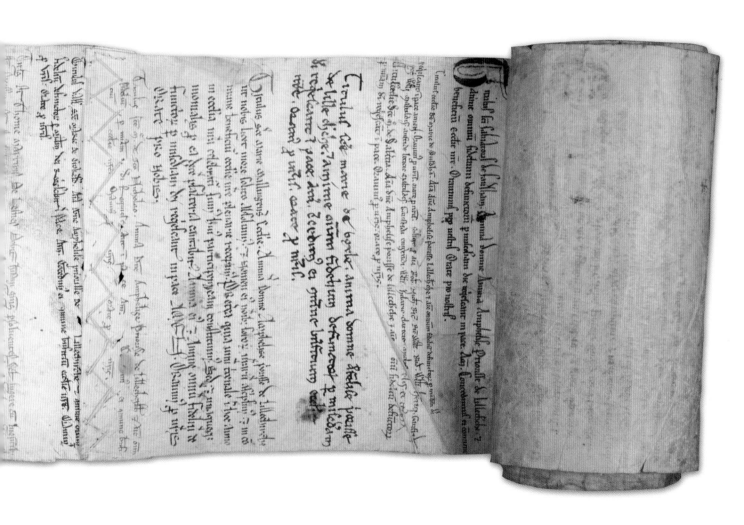

An Infant University

Exemption from rent assessment on behalf of two hostels, 1246. St John's College Archives D3.58

Traditionally, the University of Cambridge is said to have been founded in 1209, but its early history is obscure and only very thinly recorded. In earlier times this obscurity allowed all sorts of fanciful theories to develop, tracing the University's origins back before the Norman Conquest, conjuring up a flourishing, wholly fictitious educational institution during the reigns of King Arthur and of Sigebert, King of the East Angles (d. *c.* 634), and, indeed, long before. This process was helped by forged documents, scholarly ambition and a good deal of imagination. The truth, however, is much more prosaic. This document, dating from 1246, is the earliest surviving record of a corporate act by the University. Through this deed, the Chancellor and regent masters of the University granted exemption from rent assessment on two hostels belonging to St John's Hospital. The document bears the individual seals of the regent masters.

The two principal officials of Cambridge University in the first half of the thirteenth century, apart from the Chancellor, were known as proctors or rectors. These officers were responsible to the governing body of the University, the Chancellor and its 'regent', or actively lecturing masters of arts, for securing a fair assessment of the rent that scholars were obliged to pay for their lodgings. If for any reason a landlord sought exemption from this assessment, the University would need to record the fact, and we owe this deed of 1246 to the requirement for keeping good records. The Hospital of St John the Evangelist, predecessor of the College, owned the nearby church of St Peter and two houses in the churchyard which belonged with it. For these houses, probably connected anciently with the service of the church, the Hospital sought exemption from assessment. The deed agreeing to this bears the remains of six seals and the tag for a seventh: those of the Chancellor, Hugh de Hottun, and six regent masters.

Here we really are back at the start of things: the deed was drawn up before the University possessed a corporate seal, so the seals of its individual representatives witnessed and gave authority to a primitive corporate decision. As far as can be ascertained the seals display (from top to bottom): a scholar or priest reading or lecturing, a scholar or priest in a niche displaying an open book, a wyvern (a mythical beast with a dragon's head, a reptilian body and a pointed tail), a scholar or priest holding a closed book, the Virgin Mary and the Infant Jesus, and a scholar or priest at prayer.

Hugh de Hottun is, consequently, one of the earliest Chancellors of the University now identifiable.

Malcolm Underwood

Sciant omnes quod hanc literas visuri et audituri quod Magister Ranulfus de Hotun Cancellarius universitatis Cantebrigie et omnis ibidem regentes ad instanciam et peticionem Reverendi patris Hugonis de dei gracia Elyensis episcopi concesserunt magistro et fratribus hospitalis sancti Johannis Cantebrigie ad sustentacionem infirmorum qui defuncti ibidem tam in lectis quam in sepulturis eorum, ut sine vexacione aliqua facienda liceat eis duas domos officium habitabiles suas etiam tam per et portam de Trumpton quicquid et etiam quicumque ut sine et posseti libere pro eorum voluntate locare. In cuius rei testimonium predictus Cancellarius et Magister Gerardus de Thyngha Archidiaconus Carlete et magistri Galfridus de Keningtona et magister Garner et magister Johannes de Lyndeseya et magister G. de Lameseya et magistri P. de Grymmesby pro se et omnibus aliis huic scripto Sigilla sua apposuerunt. Sceleratus anno domini Mo CCo XVo

A History of the World in Pictures

The 'Holland Psalter', a psalter with Bible pictures, late fourteenth-century text with thirteenth-century illuminated illustrations. St John's College MS K.26

From folio twenty-six onwards this volume consists of a nice if unremarkable fourteenth-century psalter, or collection of psalms. The principal interest lies in what comes before: twenty-five leaves of magnificent, full-page pictures, dating from the middle of the thirteenth century and telling the biblical and devotional story from God's creation of living creatures to the death and coronation of the Blessed Virgin Mary. Although clearly not intended to complement this particular work, the illuminations run in a sequence familiar from other psalters of the later Middle Ages, and are designed to set the psalms, as Paul Binski says, 'in their logical poetic and spiritual relation to the narrative of the Fall and Redemption of Man'.

No one now knows how, or why, the earlier images were matched up and bound with the later text. All we can say, from dates of births and deaths in the Calendar incorporated in the work, is that the psalter belonged to the prominent Holland family, perhaps to the young favourite of Richard II, Thomas Holland, Duke of Surrey and Earl of Kent, before his death in 1400.

The pictures are unusual in their completeness, scale and form. They are the work of perhaps two English illuminators, possibly more, and have similarities with those in a number of important Apocalypse manuscripts, but their precise date and relation to these contemporary works remain mysterious. In terms of composition they are 'active' images, full of movement and variety, and with many unexpected details. Following the Book of Genesis, Adam and Eve tangle with a distinctly female serpent (its hair neatly gathered in a net) in the Garden of Eden, Cain strikes down Abel with a jawbone, and in a particularly dramatic image God spares Isaac as Abraham prepares to sacrifice his son. In a depiction of Noah's Ark that is at once charming and grim, beasts of every kind peer out from the vessel while drowned victims of the Flood float below. A strong sequence follows Christ's life and ministry, culminating in the Last Supper, a graphic betrayal by Judas in which swords and maces fly, the Crucifixion, burial and Ascension. In the final picture, which shows a bearded King David sitting on a cushioned seat and playing his harp, a small and rather chubby dog listens appreciatively.

The volume was presented to the College by Charles Baker in 1671 and carries a memorial notice for Francis Leeke, a member of St John's and Master of Southwell School, who died in 1670. The name 'William Leeke' at the end of the volume suggests that it was for some time in the possession of the Leeke family.

Mark Nicholls

....

Opposite: God prevents the sacrifice of Isaac, fo. 10r. Overleaf: Noah building and boarding the Ark, fos 7v and 8r.

De temptacioue abraham. 7 inolacioue arieal. Ge. xviij.

Noe fabricans archam. Ge. VI.

ingressu noe i arcta cu filiis suis. Ge. vij.

An Object of Devotion

Osculatory in ivory, early fourteenth century

An osculatory is an object of ritual religious veneration, something that is kissed, most commonly by priest and congregation during the Mass to indicate a Church bound together in charity. This elegant ivory representation of the Crucifixion, measuring just 140mm in height, dates from the fourteenth century and was almost certainly made in France. The Virgin Mary and St John the Evangelist are shown in high relief, beneath a cusped arch with foliate corbels and below a pointed gable carved with a trefoil, or decoration consisting of three leaves, in the spandrel, the space above the arch at the very top of the artefact. The upper leaf of the trefoil is pierced

with a hole, through which runs a particularly charming medieval survival, a string woven from yellow linen and gold metal thread. This would have allowed the osculatory to be suspended from vestments or possibly from a cord about the neck. A discreet socket at the base suggests that it might have been stored or displayed upright, either at the time of its original use or – more probably – at some later date.

Ivory is soft and easily carved, encouraging the skilled craftsman to display remarkable detail in his work. Note, for example, the undulating terrain at the foot of the cross; the toes delicately depicted on the bare feet of Christ; the drained, bony arms; the grain and the twist of wood in the cross; and the wonderful folding of cloaks. The latter feature in particular seems to lift figures from a contemporary manuscript illumination, animating them all in a very modern 3D.

As objects of everyday devotion, osculatories are in themselves not uncommon, particularly at this point in the later Middle Ages. The subject matter, moreover, is common to several survivals from this time. However the particular design of this example – with its single panel beneath a gabled top – is striking, indeed handsome, and seldom found. In 1951 this osculatory was purchased at auction and presented to the College by George Udny Yule, a Fellow and eminent statistician with a particular interest in the devotional culture of fourteenth and fifteenth-century Europe. Yule's impressive collection of editions of the *De imitatio Christi* ('The imitation of Christ') by Thomas à Kempis, an immensely popular late-medieval work, includes a number of scarce early volumes and stands as yet another of the Library's many treasures.

Mark Nicholls

Left: Woodcut from a 1489 edition of De imitatio Christi, *from the Yule Collection.*

39

The Laws of the Land

The Statutes of England, from Henry III to Richard II, 1390s. St John's College MS A.7

MS A.7 is an exceptionally fine example of one of the commonest types of medieval law book, which consisted of compilations of what we now know as the Statutes of the Realm. Manuscripts of the Statutes were usually small, utilitarian books, often put together by lawyers themselves, and annotated or supplemented by them in the course of their day-to-day activities; but occasionally de luxe copies were professionally produced, designed to reflect the wealth and prestige of some high-status owner. It is not known for sure who this might have been in the case of MS A.7. What seems to have been an early mark of ownership on the flyleaf has been obliterated, and there is no record of how or when the Library acquired the book. We do, however, know that it must have been compiled in the last decade of the fourteenth century, and such clues as there are point towards the possibility that the reigning monarch, Richard II, was its earliest owner.

At the core of every copy of the Statutes were the ancient pre-Parliamentary enactments known as the *statuta vetera*, beginning always with the Magna Carta (1215) and the Charter of the Forest (1217), followed by the later thirteenth-century statutes of Merton, Marlborough, Westminster, Gloucester and so on – the foundations of the English common law. These, and all subsequent instruments, were typically arranged under the reigns of the successive monarchs in which they were enacted, a feature emphasised in MS A.7 by the inclusion of five superbly executed miniatures showing Henry III, the first three Edwards, and Richard II, all enthroned, with their respective coats of arms in the borders.

Manuscripts of this type were generally the work of more than one craftsman, and in this case the scribe responsible for copying the text left spaces for the miniatures and handed the book over to a painter or 'limner' (illuminator) to insert these and other decorative features, such as the coloured and gilded initial letters that mark the beginning of each statute. A tiny note of the cost of the miniatures – they were priced at eight shillings each – is tucked away at the foot of the first page of the Magna Carta section of the manuscript.

The latest statute for which the scribe had an exemplar was dated to the twelfth year of Richard II's reign, 1388–9, so it is natural to assume that the manuscript was executed soon after this date. Richard's throne was usurped by his cousin Henry Bolingbroke, Duke of Lancaster, in October 1399, and he was found dead at Pontefract Castle, probably murdered, in February 1400. The miniature in MS A.7 shows Richard in his heyday, a splendidly enthroned monarch, known to have been a cultivated man with a taste for lavish material objects, being presented with a book by a kneeling cleric. But what is the book? The most straightforward explanation is that it must be the very manuscript that contains the picture itself, by any reckoning a gift fit for a king.

Richard Beadle

Opposite: Edward II enthroned, fo. 53r. **Left inset:** *Richard II receiving a book from a priest, fo. 133r.*

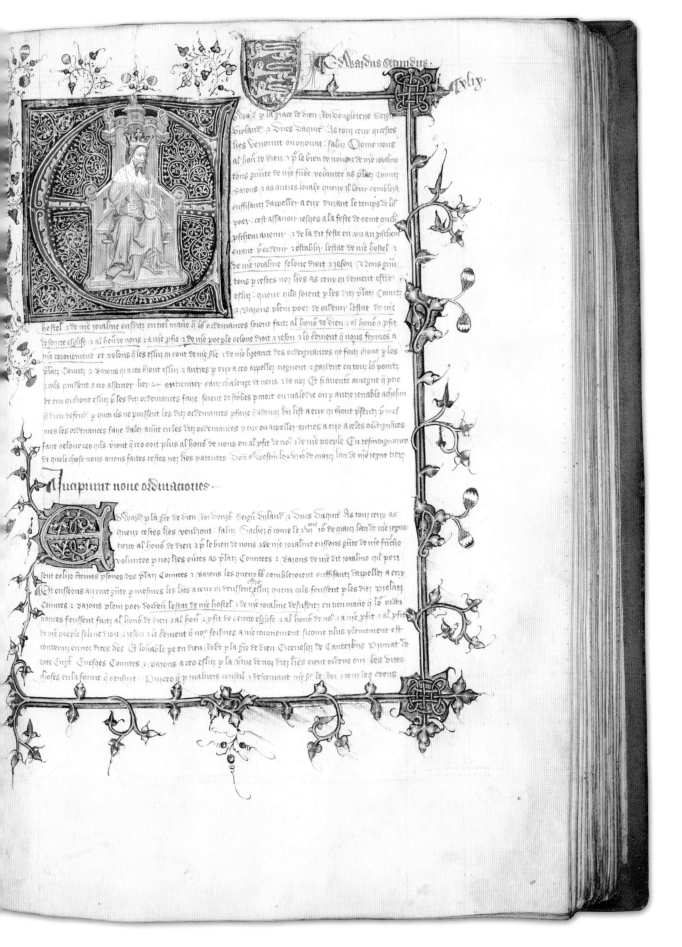

Edward p la grace de Dieu Roi dengleterre Seign
Irlan et Ducs Daquit. As tou ceux qi cestes
lettres verrount ou orrount. saluz. Come nous
al hon de Dieu et p le bien de nous et de nostre roialme
eussions grante de nostre franche volunte as prelatz Countes
Barons et as autres loialx queux il lour semblereit
suffisant dappeller a eux durant le temps de lour
poeir cest assauoir iesques a la feste de seint Michel
prochein auenir et de la dit feste en vn an prochein
ensuant pour enoiny et establir lestat de nostre hostel et
de nostre roialme selone droit et reson et nous grant
tons p cestes noz lettres as ceux qi serront estioez
esliz queux qils soient p les ditz prelatz Countes
et Barons plein poeir de ordeiny lestat de nostre
hostel et de nostre roialme en ssiz en tiel maniere q les ordenances soient fait al honor de Dieu et al honor et profit
de seinte esglise et al honor de nous et de nostre profit et de nostre poeple selone droit et reson et le serment q nous feismes a
nostre coronement et volons q les estiz qi sont de nostre frie et de nostre ligeance des ordenances qe faitz serront p les
prelatz Countes et Barons qi a ceo serront estiz et autres p eulx a ceo appellez tiegnent et gardent en tout lo pointz
qils puissent a ceo assentez seit et entenduz eanz chalenge de nous et de noz et si aucune amesne q ptie
de eux qi serront estiz et les ditz ordenances faire seroient destoubes p mort ou maladie ou p autre resnable achesun
qe Dieu defende p quoi ils ne puissent les ditz ordenances pfaire q adonqs vn sit a eux qi seront psentz p mes
mes les ordenances faire salez auint en les ditz ordenances p eux ou appellez autres a eux a celes ordenances
faire selone ceo qils vient q ceo soit plus al honor de nous ou al pfit de nous et de nostre poeple En tesmoignance
de quele chose nous auons faites cestes noz lettres patentes Don a Westm le xvi io de marz lan de nostre regne tierz

Incipiunt noue ordinaciones·

Edward p la gce de Dieu Roi dengl Seign Irland et Ducs Daquit As touz ceux qi
cestes lettres verrount salu. Sache q come le Roi io de marz lan de nostre regne
tierce al honor de Dieu et p le bien de nous et de nostre roialme eussons grante de nostre franche
volunte a noz lettres ouertes as prelatz Countes et Barons de nostre dit roialme qil por
sent eslire certeins psones les prelatz Countes et Barons les queux lor semblereient suffisantz dappeller a eux
et eussons auxint grante q mesmes les lettres a ceux qi fuissent eslitz queux qils fuissent p les ditz prelatz
Countes et Barons plein poeir desoeir lestat de nostre hostel et de nostre roialme desisortz en tien maniere q les ordei
nances fuissent faitz al honor de Dieu et al honor et profit de seinte esglise et al honor de nous et a nostre profit et al profit
de nostre poeple selone droit et reson et le serment q nous feismes a nostre coronement sicome plus plenement est
contenu en noz dites lettres El onorable pe en Dieu Robt p la gce de Dieu Ercenesq de Canterburs Primat de
tote Engl Eueesqes Countes et Barons a ceo eslitz p la vtue de noz ditz lettres eient ordene ent les dites
choses en la forme q ensuit Primero q p maniers conseil et deferment nostre sire le Roi et toutz les eyens

The Wikipedia of its Day

Ranulf Higden, *Polychronicon*, translated by John Trevisa, copy from the early fifteenth century.
St John's College MS H.1

The vast *Polychronicon* of the Chester monk Ranulf Higden, begun in 1327, was effectively the *Encyclopaedia Britannica*, or perhaps now the Wikipedia, of its day. MS H.1 contains a copy of the English translation made by the Oxford don John Trevisa in 1389. A copy of the Latin original of the work is also to be found in the Library, as MS A.12. The basic framework of the *Polychronicon* is that of a universal narrative history, from God's creation of the world down to the compiler's own era, but the work also ranges over many other extended fields of knowledge that have since become distinct academic disciplines: natural and physical science, geography, ethnography, anthropology, theology, social and intellectual history, and so on. Even the relatively limited medieval conceptions of such things, when digested, make for a very big book indeed. MS H.1 runs to some 560 large folio pages, neatly written in double columns, in the best English Gothic book hand of the time. Innumerable subdivisions of the text, marked by illuminated and flourished initial letters, are linked to elaborate indexes placed at the front of the book.

The manuscript as a whole is an excellent example of top-quality London book production in the early fifteenth century, when the English language (especially in translations from Latin and French) first came to be widely used in literary texts. We do not know his name, but work by the prolific and amazingly consistent scribe of H.1 was much in demand by the few who could afford his products, and his hand has been noted in a number of other manuscripts of similar appearance, including an early example of William Langland's *Piers Plowman*, two copies of Geoffrey Chaucer's *Canterbury Tales*, and no fewer than six copies of John Gower's lengthy collection of moralised tales, the *Confessio amantis*. Copying out long books beautifully and accurately for a living, day in and day out, was by any reckoning a demanding occupation. At the end of one of his Gowers – and perhaps his last – our scribe signed off with an apparently heartfelt colophon: 'Deo gracias [Thank God], and then oh no more!'

The translator of the *Polychronicon*, John Trevisa, was a Fellow of the same Oxford college as the heretical theologian John Wyclif, and he probably had a hand in the earliest English translation of the Bible, carried out under Wycliffite or 'Lollard' auspices in the closing decades of the fourteenth century. Trevisa occasionally inserts learned matter of his own into Higden's work. He was particularly interested in interpretations of the structure of Noah's Ark from the description given in the Bible, the relevant text being accompanied by two annotated illustrations in MS H.1.

An inscription on the flyleaf notes that the manuscript was given to the College Library in 1674 by a 'Mr Baile de Newington' in Middlesex, who has yet to be identified.

Richard Beadle

Opposite: The first folio, with an initial D depicting a knight and a clerk.
Overleaf: The nature of Noah's Ark following the description in Genesis, fos 80v-81r.

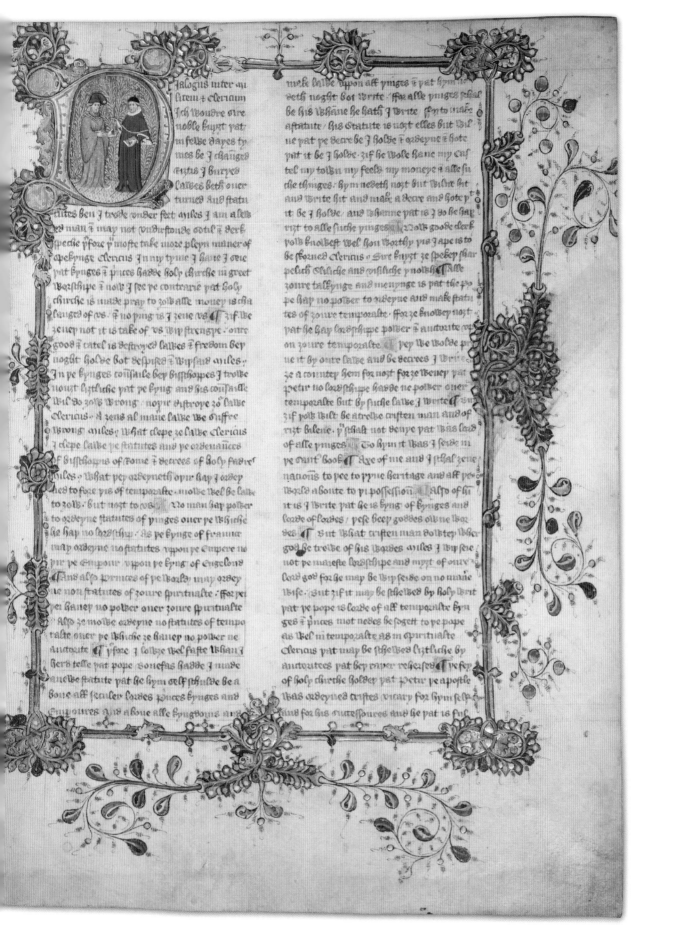

Dialogus inter militem & clericum

Ich wondre ofire
noble kuyƺt þat
in felle dayes ty-
mes be & chaunged
fiƺtes & buryes
lawes beth ouer-
turned and statu-
tes ben & trode onder feet ayles I am a les-
ed man & may not vndirstonde sotil & derk
speche þfore y moste take more pleyn maner of
spekynge Clericus In my tyme I haue I seie
þat kynges & prices hadde holy chirche in greet
worschipe & now I se þe contrarie þat holy
chirche is made pray to ƺow alle mone is cha-
lenged of vs & no þing is I ƺeue vs ƺif we
ƺeue not it is take of vs wiþ strengþe oure
good & catel is destroyed lawes & fredom beþ
nouƺt holde bot despised & wiþsaid ayles
In þe kynges counsaile beþ bisschoppes I trowe
nouƺt liƺtliche þat þe kyng and his counsaille
wil do ƺow wrong noyþ distroye ƺo lawe
Clericus Aƺens al mane lawe we suffre
strong ayles What clepe ƺe lawe Clericus
I clepe lawe þe statutes and þe ordenances
of bisschoppes of rome & decrees of holy fadres
whiles What þey ordeyneth oþir hay I ordeyneth to fore þis of temporalte moþe wel be lawe
to ƺow but noƺt to vs No man hay power
to ordeyne statutes of þinges ouer þe whiche
he hay no lordschip As þe kynge of fraunce
may ordeyne no statutes vppon þe empere no
þir þe emperour vppon þe kyng of engelond
And also princes of þe world may ordeyne no statutes of ƺoure spiritualte for þei
þei hauey no power ouer ƺoure spiritualte Also
also ƺe moþe ordeyne no statutes of temporalte ouer þe whiche ƺe hauey no power ne
autorite þfore I lowþe wel faste whan I
herd telle þat pope bonefas hadde I made
a newe statute þat he hym self schulde be a-
boue all seculer lordes princes kynges and
emperoures and aboue alle kyngdoms an

make lawe vppon all þinges & þat hym nedeth noƺt bot write ffor alle þinges schal
be his whane he hath I write ƺit to make
a statute his statute is noƺt elles but wil-
ne þat þe dere be & holde & ordeyne & hote
þat it be I holde ƺif he wole haue my castel my tolþn my feeld my moneye & alle si-
the thynges hym nedeth noƺt but wilnt hit
and write hit and make a dere and hote þ
it be I holde and whanne þat is I ƺo be hay
riƺt to alle suche þinges Now goode clerk
þou knolbest wel hon worthly þis I ape is to
be scorned Clericus o Sir kuyƺt ƺe spekeþ shar-
pelich sliliche and visiliche p nolih Alle
ƺoure talkynge and menynge is þat þe pope hay no power to ordeyne and make statutes of ƺoure temporalte for ƺe knolbeþ noƺt
þat he hay lordschipe power & autorite vpon ƺoure temporalte þey we wolde p
ne it by oure lawe and be secrees I write
ƺe a cuntrey hem for noƺt for ƺe weney þat
petir no lordschipe hadde ne power ouer
temporalte but by suche lawe I write Sir
ƺif þou wilt be a treþe cristen man and of
riƺt bileue þ schalt not denye þat was lord
of alle þinges To hym it was I seide in
þe oint book Axe of me and I schal ƺeue
naciouns to þee to þyne heritage and all þe
world aboute to þi possessioun Also of hi
it is I write þat he is kyng of kynges and
lorde of lordes þese beey goddes olbne lordes But what cristen man dolteþ observe
goþ þe treþe of his wordes ayles I wil seie
not þe maieste lordschipe and myƺt of oure
lord god for he may be wiþ seide on no mane
wise But ƺif it may be schelbed by holy writ
þat þe pope is lorde of all temporalte kynges & prices mot nedes be soget to þe pope
as wel in temporalte as in spiritualte
Clericus þat may be schelbed liƺtliche by
autoritees þat bey euer rehersed þe fey
of holy chirche holdeþ þat petir þe apostle
was ordeyned cristes vicary for hym self
ans for his sutessoures and he þat is ful

þat is in þe seuenþe genacioñ ffor lameth
was þe seuenþe from adam in þat tyme
¶ lameth his synne was I punisched se-
uene and seuenty folde ffor seue & seuenty
children þat come of hym were dede
in noes flood ¶ Oþe for so many gena-
cioñs were bytwene lameth & crist þat
payed a payne for vs alle ¶ Iosep · no
man schal trowe þat it is false þat is
I rad of so longe lyuynge of men þat
were somtyme for þey lyuede faire lyf
and hadde couenable and clene mete
& drynke & also for blisful vtues þat
þey vsede and made hem besy aboute as-
trologie and gemetrie þat þey myȝte neuere lerne but ȝif þey lyuede fyue hondred ȝere at þe leste ffor in so longe
tyme is þe grete ȝere of sterres fulfilled
¶ petrus Seth his children were good
men anon to þe seuenþe genacioñ bot
afterward men mys vsede men & wome
geñ godes sones toock men douȝtres þat
is to menynge seth his sones toock caym
his douȝtres & gete geantis petᵘs 29
and ȝit myȝte be þat Incubus suche
fendes as liep by women in liknesse
of men made geantes be I gete in þe
whiche geantes gretnesse of herte an-
swerep and acordeþ to þe hugenesse
of body ¶ But after noes flood were
oþe geantes I bore in Ebron and afterward were oþe in Than a citee of E-
gypte & þilke geantes were I cleped
Tithanes of hem come Enachym his
children woned in Ebron of þe come
Golias Iosephus þat tyme me wiste
as adam hadde I seide þat þe schulde be destroyed by fuyr or by water
þerfore bookes þat þey hadde I made
by grete trauaille and studie þey clo-
sede hem in twoo greet pileres I made of marbyl and of brend tyle I na
piler of marbyl for water and in a

piler of tyle for fuyre ffor hit scul-
de I saued in þat mane to helpe man
¶ þe selp þat þe piler of stoon staped
flood and is ȝit in Siria   pame
Noe was fyue hondred ȝere olde be g
Sem Cham & Iapheth þat is to mene
whan he was so olde he hadde þese
sones I gete and he made þe schippe
hondred ȝere afterward of tymber
ned wel smethe and was I gelued by
tyme ¶ þe schippe was þre hondred
to long and fifty Cubite broos & þi
cubite high from petule to þe haunse
der þe cabans and housynge Noe ma
a wyndolb in his schippe and aboue ou
side doutward & housynge & cabans
syns florynge þe wyndolb was ati
hisþe

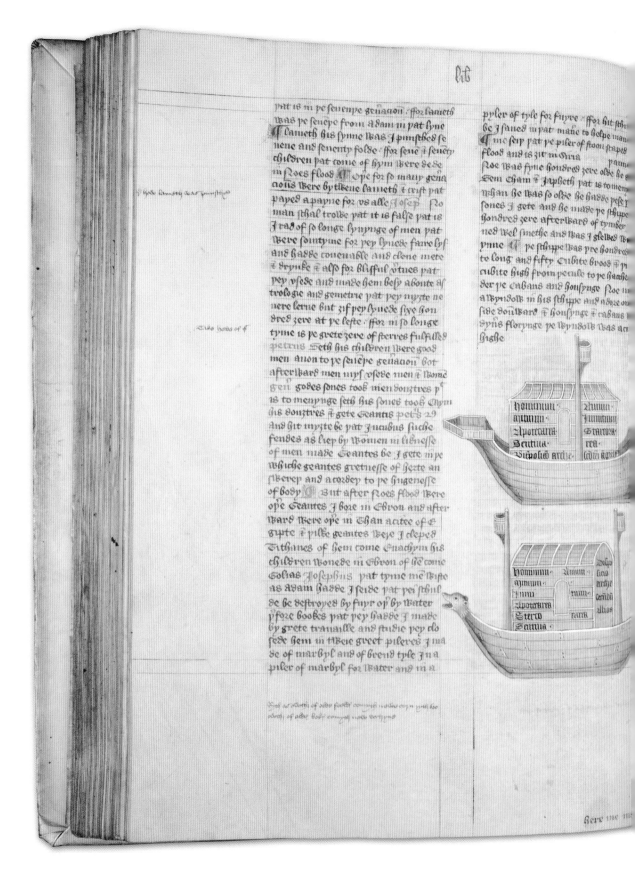

44

Here men may wondre how þe wyndowe
was I made byneþe in þe side of the
ppe for comynge of water. Doctor de lyra
neþ þis doute and þat þere we haueþ fe
stra þat is a fenestre and a wyndow þe let
of hebrewe hatte lucerna þat is a lanterne
d som men seiþ þat þe lanterne was a car
cle oþer som oþer precious stoon þat schoon
f liȝt clere I now þere it was I sette. ¶ Bot
oþer seiþ þat þe wyndowe was an hool cris
stoon and feng þe liȝt and hilde out water
eny oþer wyndowes were in þe schippe & so
nedede for schippe was ful grete & huge &
þyn ful many bestes Petrus 30 // þis schip
as I made somdel to þe liknesse of mannes body
e whiche þe lengþe from þe sole of þe foot
e cop of þe heued is suche sixe as þe brede
t is from þe myddel of þe side ribbes in þe oþ
e ¶ Also in þe lengþe is suche ten as þe dep
esse þat streccheþ from þe ribbe to þe wombe
ersa yf þe man is ful schape as he schulde
e noþer to greet noþer to smal. hugo de arm
s schippe myȝte nouȝt fonge so meny bestes
oþer þinges and so grete but þe cubites we
cubites of gemetrie. ffor þe comon cubite þat
e vseþ conteyneþ but a foot & an half þat is
e spannes. a spanne streccheþ from þe ende
f þe þombe to þe ende of þe myddel fynger whan
e hond is I strauȝt. ¶ But a cubite of geme
rie conteyneþ sixe comon cubites þat wil be
yne foot long. Gen. // þanne whan the
schippe was I made Noe in þe ȝere of his lyf
x hondred entrede & ȝede in to schippe þe firste
ay of þe secounde monþe þat is may ¶ And
ueyte dayes he brouȝte in to þe schippe al þat
he was I hote þer forto brynge or oure lorde
ent reyne vppon erþe ¶ And so þe flood was
made & occupied þe erþe wel nyȝ al a ȝere
¶ þe water of þe flood passede fiftene cubi
es a bone þe hiȝest hilles. ffor þe werkes of
mankynde defoulede þe aier so hiȝe as men trow
þ by worschippynge of fuyre þat smokede &
rauclede vp so hiȝe ¶ þis ȝere endeþ the

firste age of þe world from adam to Noe his
flood vnder ten generaciouns þat we speke
of raþer ¶ And Joseph. li[bro] p[rimo] c[apitulo] e. & also the
hebrewes seiþ þat þis firste age of þe world
conteyneþ two þowsand ȝere seuen hondred
ȝere & sixe & fifty but þe seuenty translatours &
Isidre also. li[bro] q[uinto] seiþ two þowsand ȝere seuen
hondred & two & fourty ¶ But Jerom seiþ not
fulliche two þowsand ¶ And methodius seiþ
two þowsand for here beleueþ þe odde ȝeres
þat beeþ ouer þe þowsand for þey calleþ &
acounteþ þe ages of þe world by þowsendes
and leet þat oþer deel abyde
At þe laste whanne þe water of þe flood
was wiþdrawe and Noe went out
of þe schippe þe seuen & twenty day of the
secounde monþe þat is may þan oure lorde
by hete Noe þat no suche flood schulde be
after þat & in tokenynge of þe couenant
he sette his bowe in þe clowdes þat is þe reyn
bowe Petrus 32. þe reynbowe is tokenynge
of twey domes of þe dome þat was I doo
by water for me schulde nouȝt drede hit // &
of þe doome þat schal be by fuyre for me schul
de drede hit ¶ þerfore þe bowe haþ tweie
coloures þe outer is watery for þe dome
of water is apassed þe ynnere is fuyry for
þe dome of fuyre schal be & holy seyntes
telleþ þat þe reyn bowe schal nouȝt be seie four
ty ȝere tofore þe day of dome ¶ Also þei telle
þat it reyned neuere from adam to Noes flood
¶ Also noon reynbowe was I seie al þat tyme
noþer flesche ne fische I ete noþer wyn I dro
ke ¶ ffor þat tyme was as hit were springis
tyme and þoo was I now & plente of springis
tyme & of al heleful þinges þat was after
ward I chaunged þorw synne bot after þe flood
mankynde hadde leue forto ete fische and
flesche þat raþer ete herbes & rootes ¶ Noe
lyuede after þe flood þre hondred ȝere and
fifty and he leuede in all nyne hondred wyn
ter and fifty and so deyde & lefte þre sones
Sem cam & Japheth of þe whiche þre com al

A Fine Copy of a Very Dull Book

Guillaume Durand, *Rationale divinorum officiorum*, early fifteenth century.
St John's College MS T.8

By most people's reckoning, the *Rationale divinorum officiorum* of Guillaume Durand (d. 1296), Bishop of Mende, is one of the dullest books of the Middle Ages, and by anyone's judgement, this is its finest surviving manuscript. The *Rationale* is a massively exhaustive treatise on liturgical practice. In 1372, according to the heading on the opening page of MS T.8, Charles V, academically pretentious King of France (1364–80), ordered a French translation from the Carmelite friar Jean Golein. The King's own copy is now Paris, Bibliothèque nationale de France, ms fr. 437. As with other grand vernacular texts, members of the King's family and household were then encouraged to follow the royal lead and to commission their own manuscripts of the same work. In 1380 Charles V's manuscript was lent out to his brother, Louis d'Anjou, doubtless for copying. His nephew, Louis d'Orléans, ordered a copy too in 1395. The rarity of surviving manuscripts, however, does not suggest a great rush of clients.

The St John's College manuscript is by far the grandest and most princely of them all. It was illuminated in Paris around 1400–10. One of its miniatures shows the Sainte-Chapelle, with its distinctive covered wooden staircase, a detail consistent with courtly patronage. Even in its slightly imperfect condition, the manuscript still has a total of thirty-nine sparkling miniatures, greatly eclipsing even the King's own copy with only fourteen pictures. Who could such a wealthy patron possibly have been? It is not likely to have been a cleric, such as a bishop or cardinal, since a priest ought to know the text in Latin. A tantalising clue is provided by Beaune, Bibliothèque municipale, ms 21, which was clearly copied directly from the St John's College manuscript, which must therefore have been in Burgundy around 1450.

One possible route for the St John's manuscript into that region could be through Charles V's brother Philip the Bold (1342–1404), Duke of Burgundy, or Philip's son and successor to the dukedom, John the Fearless (1371–1419). There is a medieval coat-of-arms painted on the fore-edge of the book: it is too worn to be readable, but the shadowy outlines are not inconsistent with the arms of the dukes of Burgundy.

The manuscript probably belonged at one point to Jean de Plantavit de la Pause (1579–1651), Catholic convert, court chaplain and later Bishop of Lodève from 1624 to 1648. His library passed to Charles de Prudel, Bishop of Montpellier in the later seventeenth century, who inscribed the first page. His books, in turn, descended to his successor, Charles-Joachim Colbert de Croissi, Bishop from 1696 to 1738, who bequeathed them to the Hôpital général de Montpellier, which immediately and ungratefully catalogued them for sale. The present manuscript was number 443 in that list. They were bought en bloc by one Caseneuve, bookseller in Toulouse, who was doubtless the source for the acquisition of a clutch of the books by William Grove (d. 1768), Fellow of St John's from 1716 to 1730. Grove gave them to the College in 1762.

Christopher de Hamel

Opposite: fo. 1r including four miniatures showing Christ blessing, the Sainte-Chapelle in Paris, Charles V receiving a book from Jean Golein, and Jean Golein instructing students. Above inset: Dedication of a church, fo. 22v.

Cy comence racional de diuin office translate en francois par maistre Jehan golein
de lordre de nre dame de carine docteur en theologie par le comendement du roy char
les le quint qui regnoit lan. m. ccc et lxxix.

Toutes les choses que sot
apptenantes au diuin
office tant en aourne
miens come autres cho
ses quelconques se elles
sout regardees et encerchees de cuer de
uot par diligence inquisicion sout
plantes de misteres et de toutes signifi
cacions. Et ceuleut en auer desireut le
contempler et iouir tor labondance de
douceur et de miel. Se pour ce celui qui
uueut a celle coguoissance paruenir
le doit demander et requerir de celui q
se uueut faier quel de la pierre et celle
du gat de iuer treldure quar fort est a
coguoistre la deuinte du del et les mi
sous pour ce que dieux les uuilst met
tre en terre ou mistere de leglise. Car

il est escript. Scrutator maiestatis op
pmetur a gla liquerant de la ma
teste diuine sera opprime de gloire se
pueut on dire auecic la fenie saluam
faire que le puis de ce mistere est baul
Et que nous nauons enquoy ne de
quoy nous puissons traie le celui
qui a puis puse buic et en donne a
chascun par grant affluence sans en
faire a nulli reproiche ne passe en cele
moyen des montaignes et nous en
espande par grace de iuic. Si dirons
auec dauid Hanrietis aquas in gau
dio de fontib; saluatoris. Dous puis
seres a ioie des fontaines du saueur.
et coment que de toutes les choses bai
ties et ordenees par les anciens nos
predecesseurs raison ne pueut estre

Chaucer Tells an Old Tale

Geoffrey Chaucer, *Troilus and Criseyde*, early fifteenth century. St John's College MS L.1

Though Geoffrey Chaucer is universally celebrated for the rich and varied tapestry of narratives that makes up the *Canterbury Tales*, many would say that his greatest single achievement lies in *Troilus and Criseyde*, a profound and affecting story of love found and lost, set against the epic background of the fall of Troy. Whereas there are upwards of eighty early manuscripts of the *Tales* extant, *Troilus* survives in only a score of copies, of which the College Library is fortunate to possess one of the most important in the shape of MS L.1. Though a small book of relatively unprepossessing appearance, it contains one of the earliest and best texts of the poem, and was probably made two or three decades after Chaucer's death in 1400. It arrived in the Library among a bundle of books 'Delivered in by Dr Gower July the 30th 1683', that is, from Humphrey Gower, Master of St John's College from 1679 to 1711.

Chaucer's re-telling of this branch of the Homeric legend proved to be very influential during the sixteenth and seventeenth centuries, and provided a starting point for one of Shakespeare's most difficult and challenging plays, *Troilus and Cressida*. MS L.1 bears witness to the fact that Chaucer's poem was still being avidly read in Shakespeare's time, since two early seventeenth-century hands have added numerous marginal notes and glosses, often elucidating obsolete features of the language, much as modern students do. Of even greater interest is the fact that one of these writers added a quire of parchment at the end of the manuscript in order to make a copy of the *Testament of Cresseid*, a sequel to the *Troilus* composed in the late fifteenth century by the Scottish poet Robert Henryson. Chaucer had left the unfaithful Criseyde's fate obscure. It was gruesome, and Henryson spelt it out in morally rigorous but deeply compassionate terms. His poem began to circulate as a 'sixth book' of *Troilus* in the early printed editions of Chaucer's works, and it was in one of these – published in 1602 – that the seventeenth-century annotator of L.1 found the text he copied. The fact that Henryson wrote in the Scottish language of the time means that his poem is less well known than it should be, but today's readers are now well served by Seamus Heaney's fine modernised version.

Henryson's reaction to Chaucer's ambivalent attitude towards Criseyde gave birth to a second great poem out of the first. A minor and much more muted instance of the same process occurs at the end of the *Troilus* itself in L.1. Beneath the scribal colophon (*Explicit liber* ['Here ends the book of'] *Troili et Criseidis*) a later fifteenth-century reader was moved to add an eight-line poem of their own. It echoes the sombre tone of Chaucer's ending and continues in the same vein, beginning:

Thys world ys suttell and Dissayvabull
Laughyng whith a flateryng countenaunce.

Richard Beadle

The TESTAMENT OF Cresseid.

A doly season, till a carefull dite:
Should corresspond, and be æquivalent.
Right soe it was, when I began to write:
This Tragedy, the weder right fervent
When Aries in mids of the lent
Showres of haile gan fro the north descend,
That fro the cold I might me defend.

Yet nevertheless, within mine orature
I stood when Titan had his beames bright
Withdrawen downe, and siyled under cure:
And faire Venus the beauty of the night
Vpraise, and set unto the west full right
Her golden face full bright
God Phœbus direct descendinge downe.

Throughout the glass her beames brast soe faire;
That I might see on every side me by,
The northerne wind had purified y⁰ aire
And shed his misty clouds fro the skie,
The frosts freesed, the blasts bitterly.
Ero pole Artick, come whisking loud, and shrill.
And caused me remove ayenst my will.

For I trusted that Venus, love's queene:
To whom some time I hight obedience:
My faded heart of love shee would make greene
And thereuppon, with humble reverence:
I thought to pray her high magnificence;
But for greate cold, as then, I letted was.
And in my chambur, to y⁰ fire can passe.
Thought love be hott, yet in a man of age.
It kindleth nat soe soone; as in youth head
Of whome the blood is flowing in a rage,
And in the old, the courage dull, and dead
Of which the fire outward is best remeed
To help by Physick, where that nature failed
I am expert, for both I haue assailed.

And thogh that he be com of blood royal
Hym liste of pryde at no wight for to chase
Benygne he was to ech in general
ffor which he gat hym thonk in euch place
Thus wolde loue y heryed be his grace
That pride enuye / ire and auaryce   by
He gan to fle / and euery othez vyce

Thow lady bryght / the doughtez to dyone. diand
Thy blynde and wyngyd sone ek that dam kupido
Thow sustrez ix ek yt by Elicon
In hill pnas listen for tabido
That ye me thus fez han deyned me to gide
I kan na moore / but syn yt ye wol wende
ye heried ben for ay withouten ende

Thorugh yow haue I seyd fully in my song
The effect and ioye of Troilus seruyse
Al be that they was sum distresse among
As to my Auctoz listeth to deuyse
In thisde book noll end ich in this wyse
And Troilus in lust and in quiete
Is with Cryseyde his owne herte swete

Explicit liber tercius

Pohemium quarti libri

But al to litel weylawey the while
Lasteth swich ioye y thonked be fortune
That semeth trewist whan she wil bigile
fan   And kan to fooles so hir song entune
That she hem hent and blent traitour comune
And whan a wight is from hir wheel y throwe   y
Than laugeth she / and maketh hym a mowe   whoo

From Troilus tho gan hir bright face
Aweye to writhe / e took of hym no heede
But caste hem clene out of his lady grace
And on hir wheel, sho sette vp diomede
ffor wich righte nowe myn herte gynneth blede
And nowe myn penne Allas wt wich I wryte
Quaketh; for drede of yt I moste endite

ffor howe Cryseyde Troilus for sook
Vr at the leeste howe yt sho was vnkynde
Moot hennes forth ben matier of my book
As Cryten folk, thorowe wich it is in mynde
Allas yt they sholde euer cause fynde
To speke hir harm / e yif they on hir lye
I wis hem self sholde han the vilanye

O ye herynes nyghtes doughtren iij
That endeles compleynen euer in pyne
Megera / Aleto and ek Thesiphone
Thowe cruel mars ek fader to quyryne
This ilke feythe book me helpeth fyne
So yt the losse of lyue e loue y feere
Of Troilus / be fully shewed heere

Alecto
fourth booke helpe me to find
and lore, and life y found

Explicit prohemium quarti libri

Incipit liber quartus

How to be Chivalrous

Christine de Pisan, *Epistle of Othea to Hector*, translated by Stephen Scrope, *c*. 1440.
St John's College MS H.5

Christine de Pisan, one of Europe's earliest-known women writers, enjoyed great success in French courtly circles around the turn of the fourteenth century, and among her most popular works, in both England and France, was her *Epistle of Othea to Hector*. Intended as a guide to worthy, chivalric behaviour for young knights, the *Epistle* takes a typically medieval form: legends from classical antiquity (Hercules, Perseus, Orpheus and the like) are re-told and given moral interpretations reflecting the values and ideals of courtly culture, Othea being a goddess of prudence invented by Christine for the purpose. Alongside the narrative each story is supplied with a *glose* (a gloss on its moral significance) and an *allegorie* explaining its spiritual import. The author herself supervised the production of de luxe copies of the work, suitable for presentation to her royal and noble patrons, including an elaborate scheme of illustration in which each of the 100 classical legends was accompanied by a painted miniature.

MS H.5 contains a beautifully written and finely decorated copy of the best of the three early English translations of Christine's *Othea*. Made in around 1440, it was the work of Stephen Scrope and was originally dedicated to his stepfather Sir John Fastolf, famous in his own day as a successful commander in Henry V's French wars, but still remembered because Shakespeare later appropriated another version of the name for his comic hero Falstaff. Fastolf retired from military service as one of the richest men in England beneath the nobility, and MS H.5 is typical of the kind of high-quality French style of book production that was favoured in his household. The scribe, whose elegant Secretary hand is to be seen in a number of other mid-fifteenth-century manuscripts, elsewhere signs himself Ricardus Franciscus, which probably means 'Richard the Frenchman' (or Richard François), since his work first appears in books and documents produced in Normandy. By the 1450s he had moved, perhaps in Fastolf's entourage, to London, and in H.5 we find him collaborating with one of the best-known English illuminators of the time, William Abel. Abel's work is to be seen in the first miniature in the volume, reproduced opposite, which shows Scrope presenting his book to another prospective patron, Humphrey, Duke of Buckingham. Why the translator sought another patron is unknown, but his stepfather, who kept Scrope out of his inheritance, was not noted for his largesse.

English manuscripts of the *Othea* seldom contain illustrations, but when – like H.5 – they do, the pictures are modelled upon the original scheme designed by the author. In his translation of Christine's version of the legend of Perseus and Andromeda, Scrope unaccountably substituted the name Perceval, one of King Arthur's knights, for that of the classical hero who rode the winged horse Pegasus, a feature followed in the captions that accompany the attractive picture of this subject.

Richard Beadle

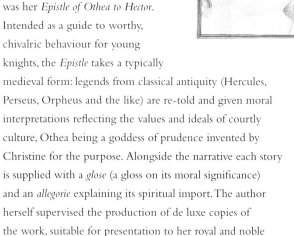

Opposite: Stephen Scrope presents his book to the Duke of Buckingham, fo. 1r.
Above inset: 'Perceval' and the sea monster, fo. 9r.

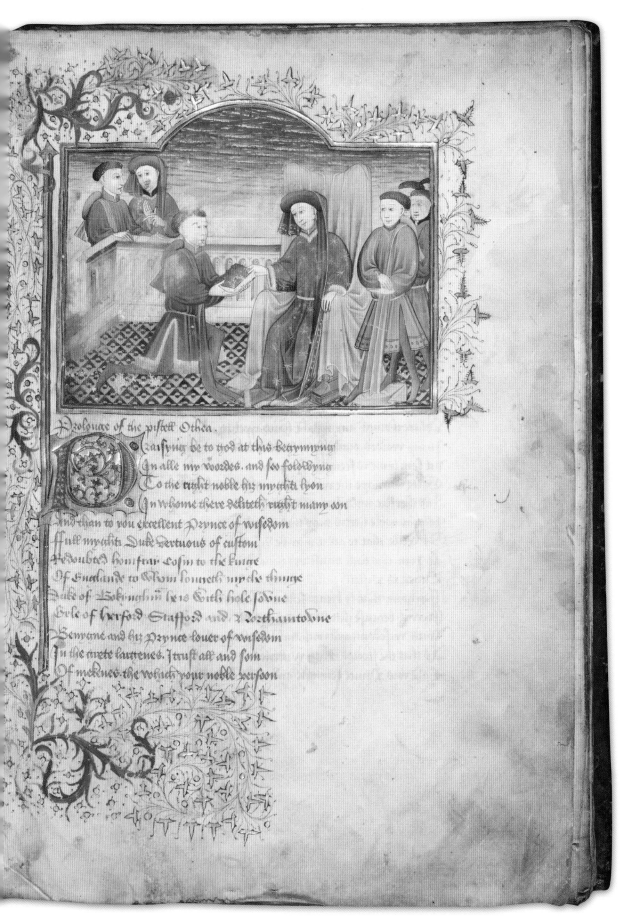

Prologue of the pistell Othea.

Pleasynge be to god at this begynnyng
In alle my wordes. and soo folowyng
To the ryght noble hye myghti lyon
In whome there deliteth ryght many oon
And than to you excellent Prynce of wisedom
ffull myghti Duke vertuous of custom
Redoubted homfrey cosin to the kinge
Of England to whom longeth my che thinge
Duke of Bokingham he is ckli hole sovne
Erle of herford Stafford and Northamtovne
Bevrare and hiz Prynce louer of wisedom
In the grete lawrenes. I trust all and som
Of mekenes the which your noble person

53

The Library's Oldest Printed Book

Cicero, *De officiis* and other works (printed, Mainz, 4 February 1466); Ambrose, *De horesto et uirtutibus et officiis sibi coniunctis* (manuscript). St John's College F.19

Appropriately, the oldest printed book in the Library has kept its original binding, and a very distinctive binding it is. Incised on the leather of the back cover is a rebus of the name Langton, and the signature 'W. Langton' appears in a book with a similar binding at the John Rylands Library, Manchester. William Langton, senior Fellow of Pembroke College in 1475, became Chancellor of York in 1486 and died in 1496. The binder is thought to have worked in London.

Bound together here are a printed copy of Cicero's *On Duties* and a paper manuscript of St Ambrose's *On the Duties of the Clergy*. As both have pages of twenty-eight lines, perhaps the Ambrose, signed by one John Phelypp, was written to match Cicero; and perhaps it was written before Ambrose's work appeared in print in about 1470. The parchment flyleaves at the end are upside down, but at the top of the first, right way up, is the longest fifteenth-century note in the volume. It concerns serving God and leading a better life, and includes a reference to Ambrose. Was Langton himself the annotator, busy reading a volume that he had designed? Unfortunately, there is nothing obviously personal or topical in the notes, which mostly summarise content.

Cicero's *On Duties*, so popular throughout the Middle Ages that over 700 manuscripts survive, was the first large work by a classical author that printers tackled. Ulrich Zel had printed it at Cologne by 1466, and Johann Fust at Mainz put the date 1465 on his first edition, which also includes the six-line poem *Tulius Hesperios*, Cicero's *Stoic Paradoxes*, verse epitaphs on Cicero, a quotation from Plutarch's *Cicero* and Horace's ode *Diffugere nives*. Unlike Zel, Fust ventured some Greek, and their texts are altogether unrelated. Fust's edition of 1466 reproduces the pagination of his earlier edition, but different use of abbreviations sometimes changes the lineation.

The latest editor of Ambrose's *On Duties* consulted sixty-two manuscripts; Phelypp's was not among them. The uncommon pairing with Cicero occurs in the manuscript owned by an archbishop of Ambrose's home town, Milan, who died in 1443. None of the watermarks has an exact equivalent in the essential work of reference, Briquet's *Filigranes*. Unusually, the catchwords repeat the last words of their page as well as the first of the next. The phrase *de horesto* in Phelypp's title, a strange misreading of *de honesto*, escaped correction by whoever checked the text against another copy.

The eight flyleaves come from a thirteenth-century copy of the Byzantine emperor Justinian I's *Institutiones* – a milestone in the codification of civil law – paved with the glosses of the jurist Accursius. English hands of about 1300 had added a few notes.

Later owners of the volume before Thomas Wriothesley, Earl of Southampton, included three named in it, none of them identifiable: on the first printed page, 'Mr Fowberye 1607' and 'Thom. Clethero'; on the antepenultimate leaf of the Ambrose, 'Edwarde Clydrowe owith this boke'. All the books that Wriothesley presented to St John's College in 1635 had belonged to a Fellow who died in 1626, William Crashaw, father of the poet Richard.

Michael Reeve

*Opposite: First page with ownership inscriptions. **Overleaf**: The colophon which dates this edition, followed by a short manuscript poem, presumably added by an early owner.*

F 19

L 20

Marci Tulij Ciceronis Arpinatis ꝯsulisꝗ
romani ac oratorū maximi. Ad M Tuliu
Ciceronem filiū suū. Officioꝛ liber incipit.
Prefatio generalis in libros omnes.

Quanqꝫ te marce fili annum
iam audientem cratippū idꝗ
athenis abundare oportet ꝑ
ceptis institutisꝗ phie. ꝓpt
summā ⁊ doctoris auctate. et
vrbis. quoꝛ alterū te scietia
augere potest. altera exēplis.
tamē ut ipe. ad meā vtilitatē semp cū grecis latina
ꝯiūxi neꝗ id in phia solū. ﬤ etiā in dicēdi exercita
tione feci. id tibi censeo faciendū. ut par sis in vtri
usꝗ oꝛonis facultate. Quā quidē ad re. nos vt vi
demur. magnū adiumentū attulimus hominibꝫ nꝛis.
ut non modo grecaꝛ lꝛaꝛ rudes. ﬤ etiam docti. ali
quantū se arbitrētur adeptos. et ad discendū et ad
iudicādū. Quaobrē disces tu quidē a pꝛincipe huius
etatis phoꝛ. et disces quādiu voles. tādiu autem
velle debebis. quoad te quātū pficias nō penitebit.
Sed tamē nꝛa legēs. nō multū a peripatheticis dissi
dentia. qm vtriꝗ socratici ⁊ platonici volumus esse.
De rebus ipis vtere tuo iudicio. Nichil enim impe
dio. Oꝛonem autē latinā efficies. ꝓfecto legendis
nꝛis plenioꝛ. Nec vero arroganter hoc dictū exti
mari velim. ꝗa phandi ꝯcedēs scientiā multis qꝫ
est oratoris ꝓpriū. apte. distincte. oꝛnate dicere. qm

Ambrosius De officijs lib 3.

Maximus eloquio. ciuis bonus. vrbis amator.
Permicesq̃ malis. ꝓfugiũq̃ bonis.
Qui sexaginta ꝛpletis ac tribz annis
Seruicio pressam restituit patriã.

Appolomius Rhetor grecus ħm Plutarcũ.
Te nempe cicero. et laudo et admiror. sed grecoꝛ
fortune me miseret. cũ videã crudicõꝛ ꞇ eloquẽtiã.
q̃ sola bonoꝛ nobis relicta erat. ꝑ te romã accessisse.

Presens Marci tulij clarissimũ opus. Jo=
hannes fust Mogũtinus ciuis. nõ atramẽ
to. plumali cãna neq̃ aerea. Sed arte qua
dam perpulcra. manu Petri de gernssheym
pueri mei feliciter effect finitum. Anno. M.
.cccc.lxvi. quarta die mensis februarij. ꞇ c̃.

Manlio torquato. flaccus. de vite hu
mane breuitate. p̃ ꝯparationem tp̃is. hoc.

Diffugere niues. redeũt iam gramīa campis.
     Arboribusꝗ come.
Mutat terra vices. et decrescentia ripas.
     Flumīna p̃tereũt.
Gracia cũ nimphis geminisꝗ fororibꝫ audet
     Ducere nuda choros.
In mortalia ne speres monet annus ꝫ almũ
     Que rapit hora diem.
Frigora mitescũt zephiris. ver proterit. estas.
     Interitura simul.
Pomifer autũnus fruges effuderit. et mox
     bruma recurrit iners.
Damna tamē celeres reparant celestia lune
     Nos vbi decidimus ᷤ
Quo pius eneas. quo tullus diues et ancus ᷤ
     Puluis et vmbra sumus.
Quis scit an adiciant hodierne crastina vite
     Tempora. dī superi ᷤ
Cũcta manus auidas fugient heredis. amico
     Que dederis animo.
Cũ semel occideris. et de te splendida minos
     Fecerit arbitria.
Nō torquate genus. nec te facũdia. non te
     Restituet pietas.
Infernis neꝫ a tenebris dyana pudicum
     Liberat ypolitum.
Nec lethea valet theseus abrumpere caro
     Vincula pyrithoo.

On the Shelf in a Medici Library

Ovid, *Collected Works*, edited by Giovanni Calfurnio (Johannes Calphurnius), 1474. Illuminated by Vante di Gabriello di Vante Attavanti. St John's College Ii.1.7

This imposing folio volume offers tantalising glimpses into the worlds of politics, business, learning and art patronage in fifteenth-century Venice and Florence. It epitomises the symbiotic relationship between early printing, scholarship, de luxe illumination and book collecting.

Containing one of the oldest editions of Ovid's works, dedicated to Nicolò Marcello, Doge of Venice in 1473–4, this volume demonstrates the passion for classical texts among the earliest printers and their need for powerful patrons. The Frenchman Jacques le Rouge established himself as a printer in Venice between 1471 and 1478, collaborating with his compatriot, the celebrated printer Nicholas Jenson, and modelling his fonts on Jenson's elegant types. Jacques le Rouge was responsible for a large number of first editions and an impressive range of texts. Many of them were written, translated or edited by eminent humanist scholars, such as the philologist Giovanni Calfurnio who was responsible for this edition of Ovid. The partnership between printer and editor reveals the contribution contemporary scholarship and the attendant perception of textual accuracy made to the reputation and financial success of early editions.

The patronage of bibliophile entrepreneurs was equally important. Jacques le Rouge's activities demonstrate the links between the Venetian and Florentine financial and intellectual elites. The illumination of this book was commissioned by the Medici family in order to emulate the unique character of a de luxe manuscript. On the opening page of the *Metamorphoses*, two cherubs support a diamond ring, a Medici device, which encloses the arms of the family's younger, collateral branch. An inscription on the last page reveals that the volume was number seventy-nine in the library of Lorenzo (1463–1503) and Giovanni (1467–98), sons of Pierfrancesco de' Medici (1430–76). Upon their father's death, Lorenzo and Giovanni came under the tutelage of their cousin, Lorenzo the Magnificent (1449–92), who helped himself to the boys' inheritance and stifled their political careers, but also ensured that they were educated by the leading humanists in Renaissance Florence. The brothers developed a passion for art and learning, and assembled an impressive library to which this volume is an important witness. It opens with a floral border surrounding their arms and a gold initial I which has metamorphosed into an amphora-like shape to frame Ovid's portrait. This pictorial allusion to the mutation of forms mentioned in the adjacent text would have delighted an attentive reader.

The design, palette and physiognomy represent the work of the eminent Florentine illuminator Attavante. He was sought after by Europe's most discerning art patrons, including King Matthias Corvinus of Hungary, King Manuel of Portugal, Lorenzo the Magnificent and his son Pope Leo X. Since Attavante and his assistants (who may have completed the initials and borders throughout this volume) replicated the same designs over three decades, it is difficult to date his works on stylistic grounds. The illumination of this Ovid might have been commissioned by Lorenzo the Magnificent or, after his death, by his cousins Lorenzo and Giovanni. Personal ambition and political rivalry often inspired the formation of art collections and magnificent libraries.

Stella Panayotova

Opposite: 'Metamorphosed' initial I with a portrait of Ovid; Medici arms at the foot of the page. Overleaf: Illuminated capitals added to the printed text.

PVBLII OVIDII NASONIS META
MORPHOSEOS LIBER PRIMVS.

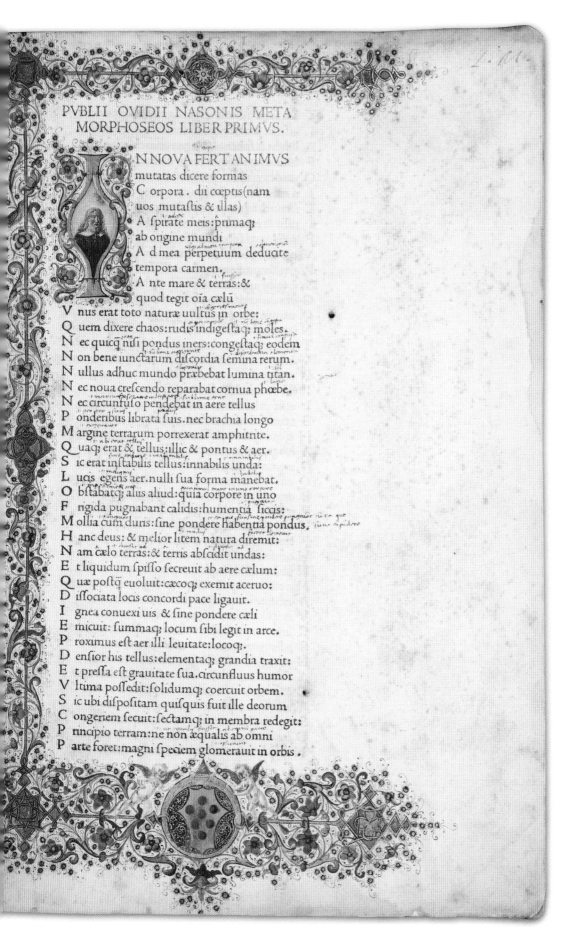

I N NOVA FERT ANIMVS
mutatas dicere formas
C orpora . dii cœptis (nam
uos mutastis & illas)
A spirate meis: primaq;
ab origine mundi
A d mea perpetuum deducite
tempora carmen.
A nte mare & terras: &
quod tegit oia cælū
V nus erat toto naturæ uultus in orbe:
Q uem dixere chaos: rudis indigestaq; moles.
N ec quicq nisi pondus iners: congestaq; eodem
N on bene iunctarum discordia semina rerum.
N ullus adhuc mundo præbebat lumina titan.
N ec noua crescendo reparabat cornua phœbe.
N ec circunfuso pendebat in aere tellus
P onderibus librata suis. nec brachia longo
M argine terrarum porrexerat amphitrite.
Q uaq; erat & tellus: illic & pontus & aer.
S ic erat instabilis tellus: innabilis unda:
L ucis egens aer. nulli sua forma manebat.
O bstabatq; aliis aliud: quia corpore in uno
F rigida pugnabant calidis: humentia siccis:
M ollia cum duris: sine pondere habentia pondus.
H anc deus: & melior litem natura diremit:
N am cælo terras: & terris abscidit undas:
E t liquidum spisso secreuit ab aere cælum:
Q uæ postq euoluit: cæcoq; exemit aceruo:
D issociata locis concordi pace ligauit.
I gnea conuexi uis & sine pondere cæli
E micuit: summaq; locum sibi legit in arce.
P roximus est aer illi leuitate: locoq;.
D ensior his tellus: elementaq; grandia traxit:
E t pressa est grauitate sua. circunfluus humor
V ltima possedit: solidumq; coercuit orbem.
S ic ubi dispositam quisquis fuit ille deorum
C ongeriem secuit: sectamq; in membra redegit:
P rincipio terram: ne non æqualis ab omni
P arte foret: magni speciem glomerauit in orbis .

A me caufa data eft . ego fum fceleratior illo:
Q ui tibi morte mea mortis folatia mittam:
D ixit : & e fcopulo quem rauca fubederat unda
D ecidit in pontum . tethys miferata cadentem
M olliter excepit . nantemq; per æquora pennis
T exit : & optatæ non eft data copia mortis.
I ndignatur amans inuitum uiuere cogi .
O bftariq; animæ mifera de fede uolenti
E xire : utq; nouas humeris affumpferat alas
S ubuolat : atq; iterum corpus fup æquora mittit.
P luma leuat cafus . furit efacus : inq; profundū
P ronus abit. letiq; uiam fine fine retentat .
F ecit amor maciem : longa internodia crurum :
L onga manet ceruix : caput eft a corpore longe.
A equor amat: nomenq; manet quia mergit illic .

PVBLII OVIDII NASONIS ME
TAMORPHOSEOS LIBER . XII.

N ESCIVS ASSVMPTIS
priamus pater efacon alis
Viuere: lugebat. tumulo
quoq; nomen habenti
Inferias dederat cum
fratribus hector inanes .
D efuit officio paridis præfentia trifti .
P oftmodo qui rapta longum cum coniuge bellū
A ttulit in patriam . coniurataeq; fequuntur
M ille rates : gentifq; fimul cōmune pelafgæ .
N ec dilata foret uindicta : nifi æquora fæui

H erſiliæ crinis cum ſydere ceſſit in auras .
H anc manibus notis romanæ conditor urbis
E xcipit : & priſcum pariter cum corpore nomen
M utat : oráq; uocat : quæ nunc dea iũcta quirino ẽ,

PVBLII OVIDII NASONIS METAMOR
PHOSEOS LIBER . XV. ET VLTIMVS .

VAERITVR INTEREA
quis tantæ pondera molis
Suſtineat : tantoq; queat
ſuccedere regi :
Deſtinat imperio clarum
prænuncia ueri
F ama numam : non ille ſatis cognoſſe ſabinæ
G entis habet ritus : animo maiora capaci
C oncipit : & quæ ſit rerum natura requirit .
H uius amor curæ patria curibuſq; relictis
F ecit : ut herculei penetraret ad hoſpitis urbem :
G raia quis italicis auctor poſuiſſet in oris
M œnia quærenti : ſic e ſenioribus unus
R ettulit indigenis ueteris non inſcius æui :
D iues ab oceano bobus ioue natus hiberis
L ittora felici tenuiſſe lacinia curſu
F ertur : & armento teneras errante per herbas
I pſe domum magni nec inhoſpita tecta crotonis
I ntraſſe : & requie longum reuelaſſe laborem :
A tq; ita diſcedens æuo dixiſſe nepotum
H ic locus urbis erit : promiſſaq; uera fuerunt :
N am fuit argolico generatus alemone quidam
M icilus : illius diiſq; acceptiſſimus æui .

The Printing Press Arrives in England

Cicero, *De senectute and other works*, printed in translation by William Caxton, 1481. St John's College Ii.1.49

The great European revolution in communication brought about by the invention of the printing press arrived in England when William Caxton started up his publishing business in the precincts of Westminster Abbey in 1476. This book, classified as Ii.1.49 and dated 1481, is thus among the earliest products of Caxton's press, and one of the Library's 300 or so 'incunables' – books printed up to 1500 – so called because they come from the cradle (*incunabulum*) of printing. It consists of a small anthology of three works on important secular themes, and in some ways it adumbrates the revival of classical learning that went on to dominate English intellectual life in the sixteenth century. Translations of two works by the Roman philosopher and orator Marcus Tullius Cicero, *De senectute* ('Of old age') and *De amicitia* ('Of friendship'), appear together with a short treatise entitled *De vera nobilitate* ('Of true nobility'), a classicising discourse by the fifteenth-century Italian humanist Buonaccorso da Montemagno.

As was often the case, Caxton issued the edition with his own preface and dedication, designed to enhance its appeal to prospective buyers. In this instance he paraded his connections with the Yorkist royal court, dedicating the book as a whole to Edward IV, and claiming that two of the translations were the work of John Tiptoft, the late, learned Earl of Worcester, while the third had been commissioned by Sir John Fastolf (on whom see p. 52). Worcester, a cultivated man and one of the earliest English humanists, had earned himself the unenviable epithet 'the Butcher of England' in his role as Edward IV's chief judicial enforcer during the 1460s, only to fall foul of Edward's adversary Warwick the Kingmaker, losing his own head on the block in 1470. Caxton's decision to print Worcester's translations accompanied by a prefatory panegyric of the man was perhaps politically motivated, a gesture towards the rehabilitation of a former loyal servant of a king from whom patronage and commissions might be hoped for. Be that as it may, it is not long after 1481 that we find Caxton referred to as the King's Printer.

Ii.1.49 was bequeathed to the Library, along with other valuable incunables, by John Newcome, Master of the College from 1735 to 1765. Before that, during the seventeenth century, it had been owned by another member of the College, Sir Thomas Fairfax, one of the most celebrated Parliamentary generals of the English Civil War. Fairfax retired from military service to his estate at Nun Appleton south of York (where the poet Andrew Marvell was a tutor in his household) during the 1650s. He read and wrote a good deal in his retirement, and this particular book gives ample indication that even an archaic, black-letter translation of the *De senectute* was of interest to him. Its pages contain numerous textual and marginal notes in his hand, and the flyleaves are filled with his copious reflections and poems on its themes.

Richard Beadle

Opposite: The beginning of De senectute. **Overleaf:** *William Caxton's colophon, and various inscriptions and annotations.*

Ere begynneth the prohemye vpon the reducynge
both out of latyn as of frenssh in to our englyssh
tongue / of the polytyque book named Tullius de senectute. Whiche that Tullius wrote vpon the disputacōns ⁊
compynycacions made to the puissaūt duc Cato senatour
of rome by Scipion ⁊ Lelius thēne beyng yong noble
knyghtes ⁊ also senatours of the said rome / of the wor-
shippe recōmendacyon ⁊ magnyfycence. that shold be gy-
uen to men of olde age / for theyr desertes ⁊ experyence in
wysedom of polytyque gouernaūce / ⁊ blamed them that re-
prouen or lothen olde age / ⁊ how Caton exhorteth ⁊ coūseil-
leth olde men to be Joyeful, and bere pacyently olde age
whan it cometh to them, And how Tullius at reuerence
of Caton declareth by waye of example . how Enneus
thauncyent philosophre purposeth and wryteth in thre verses compendyously vnto his frende Attitus also a sena
tour of Rome, how he toke grete thought and charge for
the gouernaunce of the compyn prouffyght . ffor whiche
he deserued grete laude and honoure in preferryng the
same named in latyn Res Publica kepyng the Ro-
maynes prosperous / ⁊ defendyng them fro theyr aduersa-
ryes and rebelles, whiche book was translated and
the story as openly declared, by the ordenaunce ⁊ desyre of
the nobl. Auncyent knyght Syr Johan Fastolf of
the countee of Norfolk banerette . lyuyng the age of
four score yere . experaisyng the warrys in the Royame
of ffraunce and other countrees / ffor the diffence and
vnyuersal welfare of bothe royames of englond and
ffraunce by fourty yeres enduryng , the fayte of armes

t 2

deth euery man that was there . myght lerne to dye and take his deth paciently / Wherin J hope and doubte not / but that god receyued his soule in to his euirlastyng blysse ffor as J am enformed he ryght aduysedly ordeyned alle his thynges as well for his last will of wordly goodes as for his sowle helthe . z pacyently and holyly without gruodchyng in charyte to fore that he departed out of this world / Whiche is gladsom and Joyous to here , Thenne J here recommende his sowle vnto youre prayers , and also that we at our departyng maye departe in suche wyse , that it maye please our lord god to receyue vs in to his euir / lastyngh blysse . Amen :

❡ Explicit Per Caxton

The Beggar in straw
keeps the generall Law
And when Death gives the Word must advance,
And the Guards that each House
take their place at the Louvre
can't defend the great Monarchs of France

Dum rapiunt mala fata bonos, ignoscite fasso
Solicitor nullos esse putare Deos. (1:0)

While I behold ill Fates attend good Men I am tempted to think there are no Gods.

Marmoreo Licinus tumulo jacet; at Cato parvo,
Pompeius nullo, quis putet esse Deos?

The wicked Licinus lies in a Marble Tomb, but Cato in a Small one, and Pompy
in none, who would think there were gods?

Diseases, ills & troubles Numberless
and Old Men, & with their Age increase
...painfull toyle they spend their wretched yeares
...heaping Wealth & with that wealth new Cares
...dispose & carefull to enjoy
...& suspicious in their Misanagry
...of fears & hopes, Lovers of Ease
...dy of Life, morose & hard to please
...ous at Pleasures of the younge & gay
...re they themselves now want a stock to play
...nature Censors of the present age
...what has past since they have quitt the stage
...loud Honorers of Queen Bess or tyme
...what was done when they were in their prime
...what our Tyde of flowing yeares bringes in
...with our Ebb of Life goes out again
...Humors of fourescore will never hitt
...of fifteen, nor a Boy's part befitt
...growne Man: It showes no meane address
...the tempers of each Age express.

I looke upon Old Age as a great blessing even in this
respect, that it weares out & weakens the strong fleshly
corruptions & inclinations which make us so much rest
upon this Life, and gives us opportunity with less diversion
of the flesh, to entertaine the hopes & expectation of the
blessed Estate of the Soule after Death.

The College's Foundress at Prayer

Lady Margaret Beaufort's Book of Hours, *c.* 1440. St John's College MS N.24

For St John's, the juxtaposition in one opening of this exquisite Book of Hours captures the early spiritual and educational impulses of the sixteenth-century College. A lovely illustrated initial showing St John the Evangelist at work on his Gospel faces an inscription in the hand of our Foundress Lady Margaret Beaufort, mother of Henry VII. Writing in English, Lady Margaret bestows the volume on her friend and servant, Lady Shirley, but asks something in return: 'My Good Lady Sherley, pray for me that giveth you this book.' For the devout Christian at the end of the fifteenth century, such prayers were vital in easing the soul through all the weary tedium of Purgatory towards a place in Paradise. Lady Shirley no doubt honoured the request, and for its part the College has never ceased to remember the Foundress, latterly in the Grace read after Dinner in Hall.

Books of Hours, principally designed to guide the spiritual man or woman through the prayers appropriate to different times of day, are a common surviving form of medieval manuscript. Working texts crucial to the individualistic piety of the later Middle Ages, they come in many sizes and in every quality. This handsome volume is at the top end of the range. Its wide margins, fine penmanship, magnificent borders, exquisite detail and robust use of colours all testify to the finest standards and, indeed, to high cost.

The book pre-dates Lady Margaret's College, and may indeed pre-date Lady Margaret herself. Probably written during the 1440s it seems to have been made for use in the diocese of Coutances in Normandy. Variants in the Hours and the inclusion of local saints in the Calendar provide the geographical clues, while the images are almost certainly the work of two men, one of them the so-called Fastolf Master, a talented illuminator working in France and, at the very end of his life, in England. The name by which he is known derives from his association with Sir John Fastolf (see p. 52). Heavenly stars picked out in gold leaf are a characteristic of work by the Fastolf Master, and within this manuscript, in a delightful portrayal of the Adoration of the Magi, the Star of Bethlehem shines in a series of golden rays through a hole in the roof of a decrepit stable, lighting up the face of the infant Jesus. Although much of the stable is bare, the child's majesty is proclaimed by a hanging of fine arras directly behind the manger.

No one knows the identity of its first owner, though some have speculated that the book might have belonged to Lady Margaret's father John Beaufort, Duke of Somerset (d. 1444), who was Captain General of the English Army fighting the French in Normandy during the early 1440s. What we do know is that the manuscript remained for many years in Lady Shirley's family. It was presented to St John's College by Alexander, Lord Peckover, in 1902.

Mark Nicholls

*Opposite: Adoration of the Magi, fo. 61r. **Inset left:** Detail from fo. 23r. Overleaf: Lady Margaret Beaufort seeks the prayers of her lady in waiting, in an inscription facing an illuminated depiction of St John the Evangelist, fos 12v–13r.*

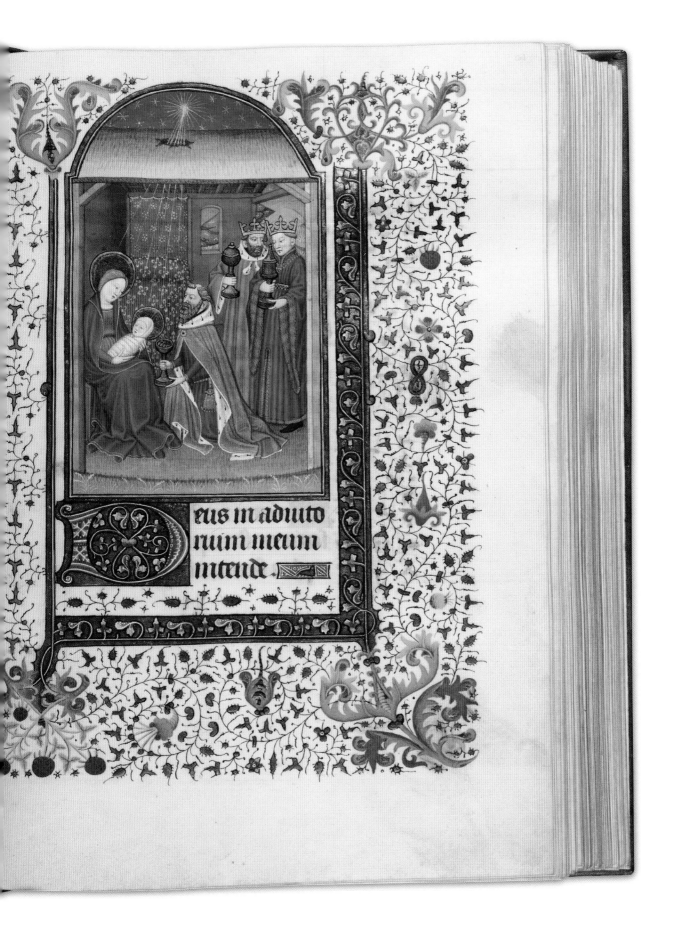

eus in adiuto
rium meum
intende.

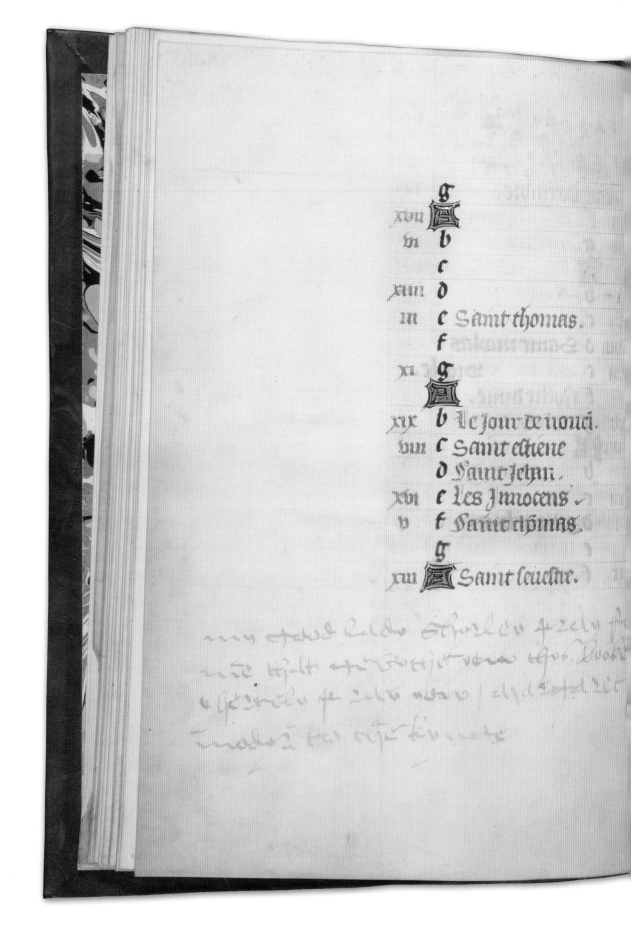

	g	
xvii	A	
vi	b	
	c	
xiiii	d	
iii	e	Saint thomas.
	f	
xi	g	
	A	
xix	b	Le iour de nouel.
viii	c	Saint estiene
	d	Saint Iehan.
xvi	e	Les Innocens
v	f	Saint thmas.
	g	
xiii	A	Saint leuestre.

Jnitium sancti euuangelij se
cundum iohannem.
Gloria tibi domine

N prinapi
o erat uer
bum + uer
bum erat
apud deū
et deus e
rat uerbum. Hoc erat in
prinapio apud deum om
nia per ipsum facta sunt et
sine ipso factum est nichil.
Quod factum est in ipso ui
ta erat et uita erat lux homi

Scotland Secures its Independence

John Barbour, *The Brus*, 1487. St John's College MS G.23

John Barbour, Archdeacon of Aberdeen, was a client and follower of Robert II (1371–90), who was the grandson of Robert the Bruce and the first Stewart king of Scotland. At some point, probably in the 1370s, Barbour began to write an epic verse narrative of Scotland's struggle for independence, *The Brus*.

As A. A. M. Duncan notes in his life of Barbour for the *Dictionary of National Biography*, *The Brus*, written in rhyming couplets, sketches out Robert the Bruce's claim to the throne and then concentrates on Scottish military resistance to two English kings, Edward I and Edward II. For many, the centrepiece of the poem is a stirring account of the Battle of Bannockburn, fought near Stirling in June 1314, when King Robert's army won a conclusive victory. Barbour evokes the sounds and the horror of battle: weapons clash together, men and horses cry out, blood spurts. But given Barbour's loyalties it is no surprise to find his narrative running on to detail the marriage of the king's daughter Marjorie to Walter, High Steward of Scotland, and the birth of the future Robert II.

The original *Brus* is an ambitious as well as a lengthy composition. While primarily a literary work, with resonances of French romances from the period, it also sets out to give a historical representation of events. When it fails to do so, as it does quite frequently, the author seems to have been led astray as much by inaccurate sources as by any literary conceit. In the absence of a significant chronicle for the period, Barbour's poem, for all its failings as a historical record, provides a principal Scottish source for the Wars of Independence. Barbour also embarked on a continuation of *The Brus,* but most authorities agree that this lacks much of the elegance and skill of the earlier verses.

No autograph copy of *The Brus* survives. The manuscript at St John's was written in 1487, probably by John Ramsay, Prior of the Carthusians at Perth, and is the earlier and slightly the fuller of only two known copies dating from before 1500. Visually it is not particularly handsome, written in a hasty, unlovely hand. Like the other early copy, now in the National Library of Scotland, it is imperfect. The first twenty-five pages are missing. Nevertheless, it deserves particular attention as a key text in preserving for posterity a fine and certainly the best-known work written in early Scots. Some passages in the complete original work resonate down the years, particularly the stirring cry:

> *A! fredome is a noble thing!*
> *Fredome mayss man to haiff liking;*
> *Fredome all solace to man giffis:*
> *He levys at ess that frely levys!*

Manuscript G.23 was presented to St John's in the 1630s, by Thomas, fourth Earl of Southampton. It was restored in 2014, the 700th anniversary of Bannockburn, with support from the National Manuscripts Conservation Trust.

Mark Nicholls

Opposite: Description of the Battle of Bannockburn, 1314, fo. 95r.

for þai trespas to god þai cry
I sall gar a thing scheu
that þou may weill þrny till of se
for doute of ded my sall name fle
now be it swa þai said þe kyng
we sall it se but delaying
he gert trump vp to þe assemble
on athir syde þai men mycht se
full mony wicht man and worthy
all redy till do cheualry

Þns war þai bowne on ayr syde
and ynglis men with mekill pryde
that war in till þai albakward
till þe battall that schir edward
conwyt and led: held frawrtis þai day
þe hors with spuris hardnye þai
and prikit apon þaim stardely
and þai met þaim richt hardely
swa at þe assemble þai
At a fruysching of speris war
þat fro a day men mycht it her
at þai meting fouronten wer
Wit stedis stekit mony ane
mony gud man born donne and slane
and mony ane hardiment douchtely
was þair eschewit full hardely
þai dang on on with þairmys þt
Gwny of þe hors þat stekit wer
fruschit and relit richt stardely
Bot þe remanant nocht for þi
that mycht cum to the assembling
for þat lat maid þt no stinting
Bot assemblit full hardely
and þai met þaim full stardely
with speris þat war scharp to stik
and dartis þat wall grundyn wer
Quhar with was rocht full mony rout
þe fiche was þai so fell and stout
that mony worthy men and wicht
throu forß was stekit in that ficht
that had no mycht to ryß agane
þe stedis men stert ayr þaim prynd

70

Christopher Columbus's First Biographer

Agostino Giustiniani (ed.), *Psalterium Hebraeum, Graecum, Arabicum, Chaldaeum*, Genoa, 1516. St John's College Tt.3.31

Agostino Giustiniani, the learned Dominican friar and former student of the mystical philosopher Giovanni Pico della Mirandola, was the editor of the *Psalterium octaplum* issued in folio in 1516 at Genoa by the Milanese printer Pietro Paolo Porro. Laid out in seven parallel columns containing the psalms in Hebrew with a Latin translation, the Vulgate, the Septuagint, Arabic, Aramaic as well as a Latin translation of the Aramaic, along with an eighth column containing a commentary, it was a remarkable achievement. Giustiniani anticipated a substantial demand and there was a print run of 2000 copies of which fifty copies, including that surviving at St John's College, were on vellum.

Apart from providing theological and linguistic glosses, Giustiniani showed himself a critical reader and pointed out, for example, that the so-called unicorn of the Vulgate must in reality be the rhinoceros. Not surprisingly, Giustiniani was an admirer of Christopher Columbus who was a citizen of his native Genoa, and he provided the first published biographical sketch of the great explorer in his commentary to Psalm 18. In his opinion the Psalmist's words had been fulfilled and the glory of God had been proclaimed 'unto the ends of the world' as a result of Columbus's discovery of America. His claim that Columbus's roots were plebeian, however, deeply offended Columbus's son Ferdinand, who persuaded the Genoan Senate to order all copies of the psalter be burned. This ban seems to have been of limited success since many copies still survive.

The first attested owner of the St John's copy is Pierfrancesco di Piero Bardi (d. 1534), a member of a Florentine merchant family resident in London. Like Giustiniani he provided glosses, but his were in the form of hand-written marginalia and relate exclusively to his personal engagement with the text. They must, moreover, be read in conjunction with the annotations in his copy of a compendium of political prophecies concerning the reform of the Church and the expectation of a French world emperor, the *Mirabilis liber qui prophetias Revelationesque … preteritas presentes et futuras aperte demonstrat*, published in Paris c. 1523. One of the prophecies contained in the *Mirabilis liber* was the *Compendium revelationum* (1495) of the charismatic Florentine preacher Girolamo Savonarola, whose brutal execution Bardi had witnessed as a youth. In 1517, according to the marginalia, Bardi experienced visitations from Savonarola and his companions which he attempted to repress. When he consulted the *Compendium revelationum* several years later he suffered a complete breakdown and passed the offending book on to the keeping of a Dominican of his acquaintance. In 1531, after the fall of Florence, his reading of the *Psalterium* made him realise that he himself was a new prophet who could guide the English king Henry VIII to the establishment of the Christian commonwealth that Charles VIII had failed to achieve in Florence. He therefore retrieved the *Mirabilis liber* and, after inscribing both books to Henry, sent them off for examination. There is no indication that his narrative was read once the books got to the royal library, however, and both subsequently left the collection, one eventually finding its way to Lambeth Palace Library and the other to St John's College.

James P. Carley

....

Opposite: Commentary on Psalm 18, describing Christopher Columbus.
Overleaf: The first seven columns provide text in Hebrew, a Latin translation of the Hebrew, the Latin Vulgate, the Greek Septuagint, Arabic, Aramaic and a Latin translation of the Aramaic.

وَالَواكراف السما منطها	וְתוּקְפֵּיהּ עֲלֵי סִטְרֵיהוֹן	& fortitudo eius super latera eorum,
ولَيسَن يحتفيوهم حرارته	וְלֵית דְּמִטַּמַּר מֵּן רִתְחֵיהּ	& nõ est quis abs'côdat a feruore eius
سنة الرب بلا عيب	אוֹרַיְתָּא דַיְ שְׁלִימְתָּא	Lex DEI perfecta
بهاترة النفوس شاهد،	כְּתִיבָא נַפֹשׁ כָּרוּתָא	conuertens animam, testimonium
الرب ذا دقه	דַיְ מְהֵימְנָא	DEI fidele
نغلم الاكعال	מַחַבְּרָא שַׂבְרָא ׃	prebens sapientiam nescienti.
امر الرب	פִּקּוּדַיָא דַיְ תְּרִיצִין	Precepta DEI recta
مستقيمة تغرح به القلوب، وصية	כְּהַדֵּין לִבָּא פּוּקְדָּנָא	letificantia cor, preceptum
الرب مضية تضيء	דַיְ בֵּרַא מְנַהְרָא	DEI purum illuminans
بها الابصار خشية الرب	עַיְנִין דְּחַלְתֵּהּ דַיְ	oculos. Timor DEI
الى ابد دايمه	דַּכְיַא קַיְמָא לְעָלַם	mundus permanet in perpetuum,
الابد احكام الرب احكا	דִּינַא דַיְ הֵימָנוּתָא	iudicia DEI fidelia
حقه كلشي عادل	צְדִיקוּ כַּחֲדָא ׃	iustificata simul.
راحة قلبه محتار ه	דְּרָגִין מֵן דַּהֲבָא יַכֵּן	Desiderabilia magis quam aurũ & quã
اشهي من الذهب والحوا	אוֹכְרֵין סַגִּי וַס מֵן	obrizum multum, & dulcedine
الكريمه وحلا م	יַהוֹר מֵן דַּבְשָׁא וּבֵרַיַה	superant mel & pinguedinem
العسل والشهد واز عبد	חֲלִיאָתָא ׃ בְּרַם עַבְדָּךְ	lactis. Equidem seruus tuus
بحفكدا	אוֹדְּהַר בְּהוֹן כַּדְנָטְרִין	est diligens in eis, & quia seruaui illa,
وفِ حفكد!	חִלּוּפֵי בְּהָנָא אֶתְעֲבִיד	propterea sic
مكافا كبر ه	טַבְהוֹן דְּיִשְׂרָאֵל ׃	benefuit israeli.
من بتذكر ضِ العثرا	שַׁלְיוּתָא מֵן יָחְבַּם	Errores quis scit,
كغربني بارد من	וּמֵטַמְרְתָא רַבֵי יָתִי ׃	ab occultis meis munda me.
حفاني ومن اللاتي لست	בְּרַם מֵן זָדוֹנַיָא פְּצָא	Sed & a temeritatibus libera
ومن الاعدا وقضى	עַבְדָּךְ דְּלָא יִשְׁלְטוּן בִּי	seruum tuum, ne dominentur in me,
ان لم بملكوا دي	הַיְדֵּין אֶיהֵי בְּלָא מוּם	tunc enim fiam sine macula,
حينبذ اكون دلا عيب اماد	וְאֵזְדַּכֵּא כְּהוֹנָא רַבָּא ׃	& ero iustificatus a peccato magno.
واكهر من عظم حكي	יְהוֹן לְרַעֲוָא מֵמְרֵי	Sint placentia verba (mearum
قول فه بكون كمسر	כַּוֵּי וְרַנְיַת רֶעְיָנֵי	oris mei, & meditatiões cogitationũ
فكر قلبي مامد ضِ كل حي	קָדָמַיְ דַיְ תּוּקְפִּי	apud te, DEVS fortitudo mea
الرب عو ندوه ومخلصي	וּפָרוֹקֵנִי ׃	& fiducia mea.

men plurium iam non nauium modo, sed claßium & exercituũ eun tium redeuntiumqʒ te ſtimonio explorata & certa. Hic puerilibus annis uix prima ele menta edoctus, pube ſcés iam rei maritime operam dedit, dein ᵖfecto in luſitaniam fra tre, ac uliſſippone que ſtum inſtituente, pingendarum tabellarum ad uſum maritimum, effigiantium maria & portus & litora, huiuſ modi maritimos ſinus atqʒ inſulas didicit ab eo, que ibi tum forte is a plurimis acceperat, qui ex regio inſtituto ibant quotannis ad ex plorandas in acetlas & thiopum terras, & oc ceani intra meridiem & occaſum, remotas plagas. Cum quibus is pluries ſermoꝛ ſe rens queqʒ ab his acce perat conferens cum his que & in ſuis ipſe iam dudum fuerat me ditatus picturis, & le gerat apud coſmogra phos, tandem uenerat in opinionem poſſe om nino fieri, ut qui ethio pum ad libicum uer gentiũ litora linques, rectus dirigat inter ze phirum & libicum na uigatioꝛ, paucis men ſibus aut inſulam ali quam, aut ultimas in dorum continentes ter ras aſſequeretur. Que ubi ſatis exacte perce pit a fratre, ſerio intra ſe rem examinans, nõ nullis regis hiſpani ᵖ ceribus oſtendit eſſe i animo ſibi, modo rex neceſſaria conficiende rei ſubminiſtret, longe

---

e. Fit cũ am uirgines nude prorſus incedunt, donec a uiris quibuſdam, eius rei peritis oſſeo quodã ueluti digito, uirginitate exuantur. Nulla ᵒac potᵒ ud eos animalia quadrupedia, preter canes quoſdam puſillos, alimenta illis radices ex quibus panes conficiuntur, haud diſſimilis ſa mbus ad oris triticeo tum glandes alia figura q̃ noſtre ſed eſui iocũdiores. Voti cõpos iam factus Colũbus, remeare in hiſpaniam conſtituit, tamen ᵉigationem, ubi primũ ad fortunatas appulit inſulas nuncios cũ literis ad regẽ premittit, qui de his omnibus factus certior mirum ies ſe le modũ gatiſus eſt, prefectumqʒ eum totius rei maritime conſtitués, magnis honoribus ornat. Procedunt & ue niẽti obuiam uniuerſi um in on ᵉoceres, magnoqʒ gaudio excipitur noui orbis inuentor. Nec mora, parantur alie naues & numero & magnitudine, priores longe exce haud lᵉ entes omniũqʒ rerum genere implentur. Mittit hiſpania iam ſua in innocuum orbem uenena, oneratur plurima & ſerica & aurata cerraſᵉ cñtis, & cui non ſatis erat de hoc noſtro orbe triumphaſſe nauigat in putos & in innocuos populos luxus, & que uix noſtram cognitam ᵉiare ingluuiem poterant ſilue euamuis inceſſantibus pene exhauſte uenationibus, in remotiſſimas plagas mittunt ſuem aprũ animaᵒ allorum ante hac neſcios uenturos. Sed nauigant cum his qui ex parata & populos iam iam captura ingluuie, proᵒ ciniis morbis Eſculapii inuento medeantur. Deferuntur ſemina & plante arborum. Nam triticum ut poſtea cognitum eſt i me uᵒ ter terre conditum fuerat, primo ſtatim ad grandiuſculam altitudinem creſcens, paulo poſt euaneſcebat, quaſi damnante natura no a cui pr ᵒ cibariorum genera, & eos ſuis radicibus eſſe contentos iubent. Soluens igitur Columbus claſſem duodecim nauium, armis uiriſqʒ les inᵒ omni rerum copia inſtructam, non amplius uiginti dierum nauigatione ad inſulam hiſpaniam appellit, oſtendit quos ui fuerat ad ceſſeᵒ irum a barbaris ſtrangulatos, cauſa pretenſa quod in eorum mulieres impudici & iniurii fuiſſent, igitur accuſata eorum ſeuicie & ᵉerenᵒ gratitudine, ubi uidet eos ad penitentiam uerſos, ueniam eis edicit indulturum modo fideles in poſterum & dicto audientes ſint. ᵉdebar ᵉ einde miſſis inglitoribus in quaſcũqʒ partes, ubi uidet iſula eſſe & magnitudine, & aeris tẽperie, & ſoli fecũditate, & ppⁱorũ frequẽ mpliᵉ

Octaplus pfalterii, Auguftini Iuftiniani Genuenfis, predicatorii ordinis, Epifcopi
dentem hebree de verbo ad verbum, terria latinam communem, quarta greca
ptam, feptima latinam refpondentem chaldee, vltima vero hoc eft

Hebrea.	Latina refpondens hebree.	Latina communis.	Greca.

| ספר תהלים א | Liber hymnorum .I. | Dauid prophetæ carmen, & regis Deo. Incipit Pfalterium A. fiue liber hymnorū fiue pfalmo rum fiue foliloquiorum. Pfalmus Dauid .I. | Δαβίδ Προφήτου σίλεως μέλος. Ψαλμὸς τῷ Δαβίδ γραφὲς παρέβραιοι |

| שרְדָאָאש אֲשֶׁר לֹא הָלַךְ בַּעֲצַת רְשָׁעִים וּבְ חַ חַטָּאִים לֹא עָמָד וּבְמוֹשַׁב לֵצִים לֹא יָשָׁב כִּי אִם בְּתוֹרַת יְהוָה חֶפְצוֹ וּבְתוֹרָתוֹ יֶהְגֶּה יוֹמָם וָלַיְלָה וְהָיָה כְּעֵץ שָׁתוּל עַל פַּלְגֵי מַיִם אֲשֶׁר פֶּרְיוֹ יִתֵּן בְּעִתּוֹ וְעָלֵהוּ לֹא יִבּוֹל וְכֹל אֲשֶׁר יַעֲשֶׂה יַצְלִיחַ לֹא כֵן הָרְשָׁעִים כִּי אִם כַּמֹּץ אֲשֶׁר תִּדְּפֶנּוּ רוּחַ עַל כֵּן לֹא יָקֻמוּ רְשָׁעִים בַּמִּשְׁפָּט וְחַטָּאִים בַּעֲדַת צַדִּיקִים כִּי יוֹדֵעַ יְהוָה דֶּרֶךְ צַדִּיקִים וְדֶרֶךְ רְשָׁעִים תֹּאבֵד | Eatus vir, B. qui non abiit, in confilium impiorum, & in via peccatorum non ftetit, & in fede deriforum, non fedit. Sed in lege DEI voluntas eius, & in lege eius meditabitur die ac nocte. Et erit tanq̃ arbor plantata fuper riuulos aquarum, que fructū fuū dabit in tpe fuo, & folium eius non defluet, & omne quod faciet profperabitur. Non fic impii, fed tanquam feftuca quam proiicit ventus. Propterea non furgent impii in iudicio, neq̃ peccatores i ogregatõe iuftorum. Quoniam nouit DEVS viam iuftorum, & via impiorum peribit. | Eatus vir qui non abiit in confilio impiorum & in via peccatorum non ftetit, & in cathedra peftilentie non fedit. Sed in lege domini voluntas eius, & in lege eius meditabitur die ac nocte. Et erit tãq̃ lignū q̃d plãtatū eft fecus decurfus aquarum, quod fructū fuū dabit in tẽpore fuo. Et folium eius non defluet, & omnia quecūq̃ facie t profperabuntur. Non fic impii non fic, fed tanq̃ puluis quẽ proiicit vẽtus a facie terre. Ideo non refurgunt impii in iudicio, neq̃ peccatores in confilio iuftorum. Quoniam nouit dominus viam iuftorum, & iter ĩpiorum peribit. | Ακάριος ἀ ουκ ἐπορεύ ἐν βουλῇ ἀσεβῶν, ἢ ἐν ὁδῷ, ἁμαρτωλῶν οὐκ ἔστη, ἢ ἐπὶ καθέδρα λοιμῶν οὐκ ἐκάθισεν. Αλλ ἤ ἐν τῷ το κυρίου τὸ θέλημα αὐτοῦ, ἢ ἐν τῷ νόμῳ αὐτε μελετ ἡμέρος ἢ νυκτός. Καὶ ἐσα ὡς τὸ ξύλον τὸ πεφυτάμ τας δεξόδους τῶν ὑδάτων καρπὸν αὐτε δώσει ἐν καιρ Καὶ τὸ φύλλον αὐτε οὐκ ἀπ ἢ πάντα ὅσα ἂν ποιῇ κατευοδωθήσεται. Οὐχ οὕ οἱ ἀσεβεῖς οὐχ οὕτως, ἀλλ ἢ ὃν ἐκρίπτει ὁ ἄνεμος ἀπὸ Διὰ τοῦτο οὐκ ἀναστήσον ἀσεβεῖς ἐν κρίσει, οὐδὲ ἁμαρτωλοὶ ἐν βουλῇ δικαίων. Ὅτι γινώσκει κύριος ὁδὸν δικαίων, ἢ ὁδὸς ἀσεβῶν ἀπολεῖται. |

pfalteriū & Citharã hoc intereffe, q̃d cithara deorfum percutitur, pfalterius furfum hoc pluribus cõflare chordis .i. decẽ
hoc fuperius habere concauitatem illã uero inferius Auguftinus uero pfalteriū fic dfcripfit. Pfalteriū eft organū q̃d ĩ dẽ
tatur pcuſſĩtis, & chordas diftinctas h̃ fedillū locū unde fonū accipiūt corde, ꝗllũ cõcauū lignū q̃d pendet & tactu refca

prima columnella habet heb ream editionem,fecunda latinam interpretationem,refpon
...am,fexta paraphrafim,fermone quidem chaldeo,fed literis hebraicis confcri
...cholia ideft annotationes fparfas & intercifas.

Arabica.	Paraphrafis chaldea.	Latina refpondens chaldee.	Scholia.
			A.

Latina respondens chaldee. — Interpretatio. I.

بسم الله الرووف الرح...
...بيد بعون الله و...
توثقه بنسخ مرا... مير
الحلط والندي... ذني...
السفر الاول المزمور ا...

Beatitudo viro, qui non ambulauit in confilio

Quemadmodum prefati sumus i pri cipio Ma thei nolumus nunc iu ftos condere comenta rios in pfalteriu ficut nec in reliquos facre fcripture libros . Caf fus fiquidem & uanus exiftimari poffet labor nofter fi poft Didymu Origene Eufebiumq; grecos, aut poft nos Hilarium Auguftinu: Hieronymus Ambro fium Caffiodoru3, aut etiam poft Salomone Abraha Dauidem & multos alios hebreos, magnamq; iuniorum turbas, pfalmos expla nare aggrederemur . At qui paucula queda adducemus qbus neo terici hebrei redargui poffint, noftri uero & delectari & in dogma te chriftiano cofirma ri quaquam que mar tyru faguine & roma nog; potificum autho ritate roborata funt confirmatione non id gent. Itaq; pfalteriu, ut a libri nomie ordi mur, grecum uerbum eft, quod latine lauda torium organum dici poteft . Eft autem ut Hieronymus ad Dar danum fcripfit, uas in modum qnadrati ely pei cum decem cordis, fecudum quod fcriptu eft in pfalterio decem chordarum pfallite il li . In cometariis ueto pfalmorum idem Hie ronymus quid fit pfal terium magis expri mit, dicens illud effe genus organi mufici mehus fonantis qua ci thara, fumilitudinemq; habere cithare fed no effe Citharam, interq;

impiorum,
& in via
peccatorum non ftetit,
& cum focietate deriforum non
circumiuit.Sed in inftitutione
DEI voluntas eius,
& in lege eius, meditatur
die ac nocte. Et erit
tanq arbor vite, que plantata eft fup
fonticulos aquarum, cuius fructus
maturefcit in tempore fuo,
& folia eius non defluunt,
& omne germen quod germinat,
granefcit & proficit. Non fic
impii, fed ficut quifquilie
quas proiicit ventus.
Propterea non furgent
impii,in die iudicii magni,
neq; peccatores in focietates
iuftorum.Quoniam manifefta eft
ante DEVM, via iuftorum,
& via impiorum perdetur.

...re pfalteriu in fupiore pte h3.Cithara uero hoc genus ligni cauu & refonas,in inferiore pte h3.Itaq3 in pfalterio chorde defup
...ccipiut.In cithara chorde ex inferiore pte fonu accipiut Hieronymo ex authoribus hebreog; cofeniut plures, & in primis Si
...ut refert cometator Salomon pfalterium a cithara diftinguit, quod pfalterium plures q cithara cotineat chordas . Appellant
A y

75

Satire for All Seasons

Thomas More, *Utopia*, Louvain, 1516. St John's College Aa.2.72

Thomas More's *Utopia*, composed originally in Latin and thus intended primarily for a learned readership, became one of the most celebrated and widely read books of the sixteenth century. His portrait of the imaginary island and the strange customs of its inhabitants was translated into the vernacular in 1551 and has seldom been out of print since, its title having passed into everyday usage. More's masterstroke was to blend satire and humour with serious social and political philosophy, in such a way as to render his book perennially engaging and endlessly re-interpretable, according to the age in which it is read. Today, *Utopia* is likely to feature as an essential primary text on the reading list for any serious university course in English or History.

Utopia dates from the central phase of More's career, when he was a successful lawyer, diplomat and public intellectual, long before his fatal involvement with the religious controversies and precarious politics in the later years of Henry VIII's reign. He completed the book in the autumn of 1516 and sent it to his learned friend, the celebrated humanist scholar Erasmus of Rotterdam, who immediately arranged to have it published at Louvain, or Leuven, now in Belgium. It was an immediate success, and soon went into second and third editions, published respectively at Paris in 1517 and Basle in 1518. A first edition of *Utopia*, however, is among the rarest of sixteenth-century rare books, seldom to be found outside major research collections. The College owes its ownership of this precious item to the outstanding generosity of a contemporary Johnian collector, Brian Fenwick-Smith, who presented it to the Library in 2007.

The 1516 edition of *Utopia* was prefaced by some intriguing illustrative material which, regrettably, is not often reproduced in modern editions of the work. On the reverse of the title page is a map of the island itself, and facing it an example of the language used by the inhabitants. The supposed alphabet of the latter (made up mostly of early printers' decorative devices) is given at the top of the page, and then used to present a 'Quatrain (*Tetrastichon*) in the Utopian Vernacular' accompanied by a phonetic transcription in roman type. At the foot of the page is what purports to be a literal translation of the quatrain into Latin, which can be rendered as: 'My ruler Utopus made me, who was previously not an island, into one. Unique among all lands, and without the aid of philosophical discourse, I represent the nature of the philosophical city to all mortals. I share my benefits liberally with others, and from others I accept without demur what is better.'

Richard Beadle

Opposite: The map and the alphabet of Utopia.

VTOPIAE INSVLAE FIGVRA

VTOPIENSIVM ALPHABETVM.

a b c d e f g h i k l m n o p q r s t v x y

Tetrastichon vernacula Vtopiensium lingua.

Vtopos   ha   Boccas   peu   la

chama · polta   chamaan

Bargol   he   maglomi   baccan

foma   gymno   sophaon

Agrama   gymnosophon   labarembacha

bodamilomin

Voluala   barchin   heman   la

lauoluola   dramme   pagloni.

Horum versuum ad verbum hæc est sententia.

Vtopus me dux ex non insula fecit insulam

Vna ego terrarum omnium absq; philosophia

Ciuitatem philosophicam expressi mortalibus

Libēter impartio mea, nō grauatim accipio meliora.

The College Rule Book

Superseded statutes for the College, 1524. St John's College Archives C1.40.7

Between 1516 and the present day the statutes or laws of St John's College, sanctioned by its foundation charter and latterly by the Queen in Council, have passed through many revisions in response to changing social, religious and political conditions. Until 1545, however, the revisions were due not so much to dramatic external changes as to the progressive refinement of an original basic code, which the executors of the College's Foundress Lady Margaret Beaufort – and particularly John Fisher, Bishop of Rochester – had drawn up between 1516 and 1518. Early rules often take a little tweaking and adjustment before they are truly fit for their intended purpose, and those governing life in St John's proved no exception.

The statutes covered many aspects of the lives of the Fellows and Scholars: the subjects of their study, the rules for their communal meals, dress, residence during a Cambridge University term, and progression through the course of degrees and Holy Orders that eventually left them fit to join the ranks of a learned clergy. But they also reached out to control – or seek to control – some more peripheral aspects of sixteenth-century life in Cambridge. Early statutes record the duty of a scholar to look after the College clock, restrictions on keeping pets, the encouragement of socialising round the common fire in Hall – perhaps the one truly warm place in College – and the regulation of classical Latin plays at Christmas. Sadly, almost all these incidentals of College life have been lost in the modern statutes, a necessary but altogether drier set of rules for St John's today.

Fisher's statutes of 1524 are bound up in the College Archives' copy with those prepared by his close colleague Richard Fox, Bishop of Winchester, for his foundation of Corpus Christi College, Oxford (1517). And it is immediately clear that Fisher's last complete code of statutes for St John's, dated 1530, owes much to those regulating Corpus Christi. The statutes illustrated here come from five bifolia (sheets folded in half, thus giving four pages each) of an early version of the code produced in 1524, perhaps compiled between 1520 and 1522. They are pleasingly decorated with various grotesque figures, including fools' heads with bells – a reminder, as with the gargoyles of medieval cathedrals, that the serious aims of mortals are always punctured by their sometimes humorous frailty. Or perhaps their inclusion was just one more way to keep the reader at his task!

Malcolm Underwood

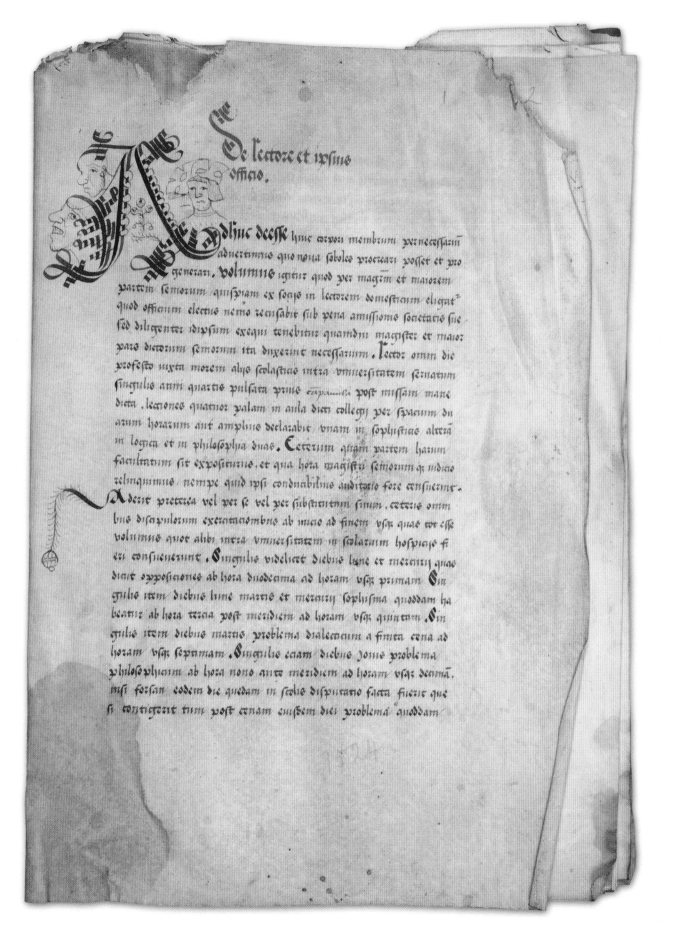

De lectore et ipsius officio.

Adhuc deesse huic corpori membrum pernecessarium aduertimus quo noua soboles procreari posset et progenerari. Volumus igitur quod per magnam et maiorem partem seniorum quispiam ex sociis in lectorem domesticum eligatur quod officium electus nemo recusabit sub pena amissionis societatis sue sed diligenter idipsum exequi tenebitur quamdiu magister et maior pars dictorum seniorum ita dixerint necessarium. Lector omni die profesto iuxta morem aliorum scolasticorum intra vniuersitatem seruatum singulis anni quartis pulsata prius campana post missam mane dicta, lectiones quatuor palam in aula dicti collegii per spacium duarum horarum aut amplius declarabit, vnam in sophistica, alteram in logica et in philosophia duas. Ceterum quam partem harum facultatum sit expositurus et qua hora magistri seniorum iudicio relinquimus, nempe quid ipsi condignabilius auditorio fore censuerint. Aderit preterea vel per se vel per substitutum suum, ceteris omnibus discipulorum exercitacionibus ab inicio ad finem vsque quas tot esse volumus quot alibi intra vniuersitatem in scolarum hospicio fieri consueuerint. Singulis videlicet diebus lune et mercurii quas dicit oppositiones ab hora duodecima ad horam vsque primam. Singulis item diebus lune martis et mercurii sophisma quoddam habeatur ab hora tercia post meridiem ad horam vsque quintam. Singulis item diebus martis problema dialecticum a finita cena ad horam vsque septimam. Singulis eciam diebus iouis problema philosophicum ab hora nona ante meridiem ad horam vsque decimam, nisi forsan eodem die quedam in scolis disputacio facta fuerit que si contigerit tum post cenam eiusdem diei problema quoddam

Keeping the Landlord Happy

Licence in Mortmain, 9 April 1526. St John's College Archives D5.4

Since the Norman Conquest all land in England was considered to be held from the Crown as ultimate landlord, but subject also to the rights of the Crown's tenants and sub-tenants, known as the mesne lords. These tenants, with the Crown, were entitled to various services attached to the land, and to taxes when the land was inherited, sold or otherwise changed hands. Grants of land to Colleges were regarded in the same light as those made to churches and to monasteries: being made in perpetuity to a single 'undying' institution they deprived the Crown and the mesne lords of subsequent profits proceeding from human mortality. The land so granted was said to have passed into mortmain, literally a 'dead hand', and so to have been lost by the lords to the institution for ever.

Crown and mesne lords understandably felt that some recompense was in order. Consequently when a Cambridge or Oxford College acquired land, whether purchased or given by benefactors, a fine was exacted from the College to compensate for the loss of profits. It was the Crown who demanded the highest price, issuing a licence in mortmain in return for a large fee, though mesne lords also sometimes issued their own licences. In the later Middle Ages, it became common practice for the Crown to grant licences to acquire properties up to a stated value, rather than a licence for each property. This licence in mortmain of 1526 was granted for £200 (about £120,000 today) to cover the acquisition by St John's of the sites and lands of the dissolved priories of Broomhall or Bromhall (Berkshire) and Higham (Kent), estates which remained long thereafter in the possession of the College. Both Broomhall and Higham were dissolved some years before Henry VIII's destruction of the monastic way of life in England in the later 1530s, and both illustrated the decline of monasticism apparent in late medieval society. At its dissolution, Broomhall, a Benedictine community, housed just three nuns. The house at Higham, also known as Lillechurch (see p. 28), does not appear to have been any larger.

Interesting in its content, the document is also lovely to look at. It has a remarkably fine initial H containing a pen-and-ink drawing of St John the Evangelist within a portico.

Malcolm Underwood

HENRICVS

Henricus ordinus dei grā Anglie ⁊ Fraunc̄ Rex ⁊ fidei defensor ⁊ ...
septimo de grā nrā spāli ac ex c̄tā scienciā ⁊ mero motu nr̄is concessimus ⁊ licenciam dedimus p nobis ...
Horneby clico ⁊ Hugoni Asshton clico cūm defunctꝰ exequtions̄ testamenti ⁊ vltime voluntatis maḡate nup ...
porciones appertꝰ ⁊ annuitates ac aduocacōes eccliaꝝ Hospitaliꝰ Prioratꝰ libas capellꝰ ⁊ alia benefic̄ ecclie ...
in capite vel alit̄ Aut aliquo alio modo siue de aliquiꝰ aliis p̄sonis seu de aliqua alia p̄sona teneretꝰ Dictis n̄ ...
habens tenens ⁊ gaudens eisdem maḡo ⁊ Socꝭ siue Scōlaꝛibus ⁊ successoꝛibus suis ꝑpetuis Et eisdem maḡo ...
⁊ alia benefic̄ ecclesiastic̄ quecumꝗ ꝓecnon omnia ⁊ omnimoda hereditamenta ⁊ alias possessiones quaskcumꝗ ...
ꝑciꝑe potuissent ⁊ tenere sibi ⁊ successoꝛibus suis p̄dicꝭ sicut in eisdem his nr̄is continetur similit̄ licenciam ...
ordinatis Aut aliqua alia māteria re vel causa quitcumꝗ non obstantibus Et vltenꝰ ꝑ litteras nr̄as pr ...
gaudere potuissent eis ⁊ successoꝛibus suis in custus suos ꝓprios in dotacōem dc̄i Collegii ⁊ augmentacōem sustentacōen ...
inde mcontinuam factis certis siue ceꝛtuis Aut aliqua alia māteria ꝛ seu causa quitcumꝗ in aliquo non obstantibus Et hoc absꝗ fine et feodo vel aliquo alio ...
maḡnificacōnibus p̄texu aliquoꝛum his nr̄is vel aliquoꝛum hr̄ium moꝛum heredum vel successorum nrōrum de eo quod sciꝑtum seu aliquoꝛ commission ...
aliis his nr̄is patentibus heredum vel successorum nostrorum de eo siue pro p̄missis in dictis litteꝭ nr̄is contentis vel eorum aliquo quo vis modo ꝛ sc̄is siue ...
c̄lus Puntoñ Epūs Johannes Roffen Episcopus ⁊ Cayolus Comes Dygeni ꝓecnon nunc maḡister ⁊ Socꝭ ar Scōlaꝛes Collegii sc̄i Johannis Euangeliste in vniūsitatꝰ ...
concessiꝰ sc̄iūa nr̄e pr̄e hac̄te ⁊ factae fuerunt eisdem Epūo Episcopo comiti Thom̄ Heuꝛ ⁊ expꝛex Johanni Henꝛio horneby ⁊ Hugoni qꝺ ipsi exequtores et ...
concederetur tunc maḡo ⁊ Socꝭ siue Scōlaꝛibus Collegii sc̄i Johannis Euangeliste in vniūsitate nrī Cantibr̄ et non tunc maḡistro ⁊ Socꝭ ar Scōlaꝛibus Col ...
p̄dicam restituere Cancellario ea intende qꝺ nos alias litteras nostras patentes eisdem Epūo Episcopo ⁊ Comiti ar dabur Supꝰtꝰ Ac nunc maḡo ar Socꝭ ...
p̄dietas nobis in Cancellariam nrām Prc̄am restituerunt cancellandas de grā nrī spāli ac ex c̄tā scienciā ⁊ mero motu nr̄is concessimus ⁊ licenciam de ...
nuenti et p̄time voluntatis maḡate nup̄ comiñs̄ Richmonis Derb̄ Aue nr̄e chaꝛissime qꝺ ipi exequtores vel assiḡ sui ac alie p̄sone quecumꝗ de ...
ecclesiastica quecumꝗ ꝓecnon omnia ⁊ omnimoda hereditamenta ⁊ alias possessiones quaskcum ꝗ eis Alexalciam intentacōem libꝛanī p̄ annī ostra repp̄sas taln ...
p̄dcā ⁊ successoꝛibus suis facere concedere appropriare consuidare amortere ⁊ vnire possint vel possit Hennꝰ tenend̄ ⁊ gaudens eisdem maḡistro ar Socꝭ ar Scō ...
ar aduocacōes Hospitalia Prioratꝰ libas capellꝰ ⁊ alia benefic̄ ecclesiastic̄ quecumꝗ ꝓecnon omnia ⁊ omnimoda hereditamenta ⁊ alias possessiones quaskc ...
possint ⁊ tenere sibi et successoꝛibus suis p̄dcꝭ sicut p̄textum est similit̄ licenciam dedimus ⁊ concessimus de āmus et concessimus ⁊ cōcedimus sꝑalem Statuto de hū ...
non obstantibus Et vltenꝰ de p̄dcōn grā nr̄ āmus et concessimus ac p̄ p̄sentes damus et concedimus pro nobis et heredibus nr̄is p̄cas p̄sent ...
⁊ alia benefic̄ ecclesiastic̄ quecumꝗ ꝓecnon omnia et omnimoda hereditamenta ⁊ alias possessiones quaskcumꝗ eis sic dcā vel concessiā appropriatā consuidatā ...
Prc̄co statuto de hꝭ et tenementis Ad manum moꝛtuam non ponendꝭ Aut aliquo alio statuto Actu ordinacōe siue restꝛione inde incontanꝰ factis ceꝛtis ...
seu concāo soluencī Aut faciencī p̄textu viginti solidos ⁊ quatuor denaꝛios taluim et non vltra Et absꝗ aliquod inquisic̄ siue aliquibus inquisicōnis p̄texu ...
ꝑpe fienꝭ capiendꝰ in Cancellario nrā heredum vel successorum nrōrum seu alibi reuensꝰ ⁊ absꝗ aliquibꝰ aliis his nr̄is patentibus heredum vel succe ...
obstantibus In cuiꝰ rei testimonium has litꝭ nr̄as fiei fecimus patentes Teste me ipō apud Westm̄ vicesimo nouo die Aprilis Anno regni ...

Mirrors for Princes

Erasmus, *Institutio principis christiani*, 1529. St John's College Aa.6.51

This 1529 copy of *The Training of a Christian Prince*, a contribution by the prominent Renaissance humanist Erasmus of Rotterdam to a genre often known as 'mirrors for princes' (handbooks intended to instruct Christian rulers in their duties), is remarkable chiefly because it is one of the few such books that we know was actually read by a Christian prince. The main evidence for this is found on the rear endpaper, where an unknown hand has copied out an extract from Cicero's dialogue *Laelius*, otherwise known as *De amicitia* ('On friendship'): *Mihi vero non minori curae est, qualis Respublica post mortem meam futura sit, quam qualis hodie sit*. Beneath this a different hand has added: 'The prince this did wrighhen hee went to schole.'

Traditionally, this prince has been identified as Edward VI, son and heir of Henry VIII. If so, the book would have been part of the educational programme devised for the young king by his tutor, the Fellow of St John's College and Regius Professor of Greek, John Cheke. We know that Cheke made his pupil copy out texts from the *De amicitia* and other works of Cicero. One could even speculate that this book might once have belonged to Cheke himself, as it was printed in the same year that he was elected to his Fellowship at St John's.

A more certain royal association is evident from the book's handsome binding, which features the arms of Elizabeth I tooled in gold on the front and back covers. Three flyleaves that were bound in, front and back, at the same time, explain why this binding was added. For the leaves at the front have been filled with a manuscript letter in Greek addressed to the Queen by the great Protestant martyrologist, John Foxe. Foxe admired the short-lived King Edward, in whose reign a thoroughly Protestant Reformation was initiated in England. For him, Edward really was the model of a truly Christian prince. Elizabeth, in contrast,

was in Foxe's view at times lukewarm in her commitment to the Gospel, and his elaborate covering letter, like the gift itself, is designed to remind her tactfully of her duties. If the book really had formerly belonged to Edward, then the implicit invocation of his memory and example would have sharpened the dedication. However, it is important to note that Foxe's letter makes no mention of Edward at all, which might cast some doubt on the traditional interpretation of the Ciceronian tag.

It is not clear how this book, having been in the royal collection under Elizabeth, made its way by the end of the next century into the hands of a London bookseller, Alexander Bosvile. Presumably it had come onto the market during the turmoil of the Civil Wars. At any rate, there it caught the eye of Bosvile's Johnian friend, Thomas Baker, who persuaded him to donate it to the College Library. Such at least seems the implication of the inscription on the front endpaper in Baker's unmistakable spidery hand: *Ex Dono A. Bosvile Bibliopolae Londinensis procurante T: Baker.*

One further intriguing thought is suggested by the quotation from Cicero on the rear endpaper. It translates as follows: 'The future condition of the State after my death is of no less concern to me than its condition today.' If this really was added by Edward, did he perhaps pen this in his last days, when he was doing all he could to divert the succession to his Protestant cousin, Jane Grey, at the expense of his Catholic half-sister Mary, whose determination to reverse his religious settlement was all too evident to him?

Richard Rex

*Above: Inscriptions on the rear endpaper. **Inset left:** The arms of Elizabeth I on the contemporary binding.*

The Magus and his Books

Omnia diuini Platonis opera / tralatione Marsilii Ficini, Basle, 1532. St John's College Cc.2.16

This 1532 edition of Marsilio Ficino's translation of and commentary on Plato came to St John's in 1680 through the bequest of a former Master, Peter Gunning. A seemingly unexceptional Renaissance humanist translation of ancient Greek philosophy, its particular significance only came to light in 2002, when a cataloguer noticed the name 'JOHN DEE' inked on the bottom edge. It was not Dee's usual mark of ownership, but could this possibly be a lost volume from his great library?

Dee graduated from St John's in 1546 and had become an internationally travelled scholar, eager to impress with the new mathematical astrology he had learnt at Louvain, when his influential Johnian connections won him a receptive audience at the court of Edward VI. His expertise in mathematics and other occult arts soon earned him royal and aristocratic patronage. However, after Edward's untimely death, when his disinherited sister Mary had claimed the throne, married her Spanish prince, and now thought she was pregnant with a Catholic heir, Dee was caught casting treasonous horoscopes for her sister, the suspected plotter Elizabeth, and talked his way out of the consequences only with a thoroughly tarnished reputation.

Nevertheless, Dee could still be useful to a sympathetic elite, and he carved out a career as an intellectual consultant, supported by the vast library he established in his mother's house at Mortlake on Thames – his 'hostel for itinerant philosophers'. Growing to over 3000 titles, dwarfing the libraries of Oxbridge colleges at that time, Dee deliberately arranged his collection in no particular order; to find anything, you had to ask Dee. The volumes themselves were systematically annotated, with key passages marked for ease of retrieval.

Dee made notable, if often erroneous, scholarly contributions to the hazardous business of exploratory navigation, seeking north-east and north-west passages to Cathay and the Orient. Believing that he was God's chosen and inspired instrument, he embarked on a misguided Continental adventure in 1583, peddling alchemy and apocalypse round the courts of central Europe. From his library he took around 800 volumes with him, mostly concerning alchemy and occult philosophy. These he marked in a contemporary catalogue of the full collection, leaving the remainder at the mercy of his many creditors. His travelling library included the copy of Plato's works, recently identified as ours.

The book bears the signature of 'P. Saunders', a physician and student of Dee's, who inherited volumes from Dee's library by various means. The annotations, in Dee's hand, illustrate how Dee used his books. Underlined passages on geometry relate directly to Dee's own published introduction to Euclid. Marginal notes and Dee's characteristic pointing hand highlight his interests in the magical power of the original language of God and man, the true names of things, and the role of guiding angels or familiar demons, which were central to his long and desperate quest for divine knowledge through conversations with the illusory angels conjured into his crystal ball by charismatic colleagues.

So, this ordinary and extraordinary volume bears witness to one of the greatest libraries of the sixteenth century, and its annotations illuminate the way that ancient and modern authorities influenced and validated the philosophy of a remarkable Renaissance mind.

Ian McKee

....

Opposite: Dee's mark of ownership. Right: Dee's annotations and, just visible, a 'manicule' or pointing hand, p. 634.

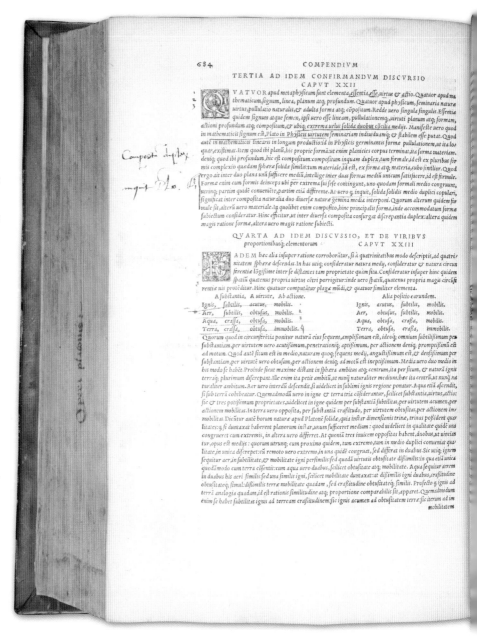

Spreading the Word of God

The Byble in Englyshe, 1539. St John's College Bb.8.30

This magnificently illustrated presentation copy of the first official edition of the entire Bible in English was one of a pair specially produced on vellum in 1539 for Henry VIII and his chief minister Thomas Cromwell. This one, which has been in the College Library since the seventeenth century, has always been described as Cromwell's, and was probably given by John Williams, Bishop of Lincoln, Lord Keeper of the Great Seal, and the founder of what is now the Old Library. Henry VIII's copy is in the National Library of Wales at Aberystwyth.

The 1539 Great Bible was printed in four parts, each with its own title page. It is the first title page (also used for part three) that has always attracted most attention, for it depicts an allegory of the Reformation by which Henry VIII declared himself Supreme Head on Earth of the Church of England. The dominating figure is Henry himself, enthroned, proffering with each hand a Bible (helpfully labelled *Verbum Dei*, 'Word of God') to his two chief advisers, who stand bareheaded on either side: to his right Thomas Cranmer, Archbishop of Canterbury, and to his left Thomas Cromwell. One level down, the story moves on. Cranmer and Cromwell, identified by roundels showing their heraldic blazons, hand on the Word of God to the clergy and the lay elites. Lower still, a priest preaches to the people. The core message of the Word of God, according to Henry, was that people should know and carry out their duties to God, king and neighbour. Their duty to their king was his primary concern, and the priest therefore preaches on a soundly monarchical text, urging Christians to offer prayers 'for all men, for kings etc.' (1 Timothy 2:1–2). Henry's subjects, scattered across the foot of the page, respond warmly: *Vivat Rex*, 'God save the Kynge'.

The glorious title page shown here, from part three, has preserved its finer details better than the one at the front of the book, and also follows the underlying printed woodcut more closely. But it is worth commenting on how the frontispiece differs from the version shown here. In the woodcut, as in the version here, Henry is wearing a bonnet and a furred robe. On the frontispiece, his bonnet becomes an imperial crown and his robe imperial purple, trimmed with gold and gems: Henry 'in majesty'. And at the bottom right, the composition is radically altered. In this version we see the prison, the destination of dissidents and malefactors. But in the main frontispiece the prison disappears, and in its place stands a well-to-do layman, apparently reading from the Bible to those around him. Cromwell was not only sympathetic to what would soon be called Protestantism, but also mordantly anticlerical. This picture signals his conviction that reading the Bible was not just for the clergy.

A set of 'injunctions' (instructions) that Cromwell issued for the Church of England in 1538 required every church to purchase an English Bible 'of the largest volume' for the use of parishioners. The Great Bible was published to supply this need, and Cromwell was as alive to the commercial as to the spiritual opportunity. A royal patent of November 1538 authorised him to stop anyone else from printing English Bibles, in effect conferring on him the intellectual property in the text, and he was a major investor in the project. But Cromwell was not to enjoy this income for long. In 1540 he fell from power and was executed. In later editions of the Great Bible, his heraldic arms were excised.

Richard Rex

Opposite: Title page to the third part of the Great Bible, 'Hagiographa'.
Overleaf: Pages showing the richness of the illustration.

their enheritaunce, and repayred the cyties, and dwelt in them.

And the children of Israel departed thēce at that tyme, ↄ went every mā to his trybe, and to his kynred, ād went out from thence every man to hys enheritaunce. ✱ In those dayes there was no kyng in Israel: but euerye man dyd that which semed ryght in his owne eyes.

✱ Jud.rbij.b. and.rbiij.a.

❡ The ende of the boke of Iud=
ges, called in the Hebrue
Sophtim.

❡ The boke of Ruth,

❡ The fyrst Chapter.

❡ Elimelec goeth with his wyfe and chyldren
into the lande of Moab.

T fortuned, that ✱
(in the dayes of a certayne
iudge) when the Iud=
ges iudged, there fell
a darth in the lande,
and a certen man of
Bethlehē Iuda wēt
for to soiourne in ↄ
cōtreye of Moab. he
and hys wyfe, and his two sonnes. The name of the man was Elimelec, and the name
of hys wyfe, Naomi: and the names of his
two sonnes were, Mahlon and Chilion, ād
they were Ephraites, out of Bethlehē Iuda. And when they came into the lande of
Moab, they contynued there. And Elimelec
Naomies husband dyed, and she remayned
with her two sonnes, which toke thē wyues
of the nacyons of the Moabites: the ones
name was Orpha, ↄ the others Ruth. And

waye to returne vnto ↄ lande of Iuda. And
Naomi sayde vnto her two daughters in
lawe: go and returne eche of you vnto your
mothers house: and the Lord deale as kynd-
lye with you, as ye haue dealt with ↄ deed
and with me. And the Lord geue you, that
you maye finde rest, ether of you in ↄ house
of her husbande: And whan she kyssed them
they lift vp their voyce, and wepte, ↄ sayd
vnto her: we wyll go with ↄ vnto thy folke
And Naomi sayd: turne agayne my daughters: for what cause will you go wyth me
Are ther any mo chyldren in my wombe, to
be yo husbādes? Turne agayne my daughters, ād go: for I am to olde to haue an husband. And yf I sayd, I haue hope, yf I toke
a man also this nyght: yee and though I had
all readye borne sonnes, wolde ye tarye after them, tyll they were of age? or wolde ye
for them so lōg refrayne frō takyng of hus-
bandes? Not so my daughters: for it greue
me moche for youre sakes, that the hande of
the Lorde is gone out agaynst me.

And they lift vp their voyces, ād wep
agayne, ↄ Orpha kissed her mother in law
but Ruth aboade styll by her. And Nao-
sayde: se, thy syster in law is gone backe
gayne vnto her people ād vnto her goddes
returne thou after her. And Ruth answere
entreate me not to leaue the, and to returne
frō after the: for whether thou goest, I wyll
go also: ↄ where thou dwellest, there I wyll
dwell: thy people shalbe my people, and thy
God my God, Where thou diest, there wyll
I dye, ↄ there will I be buried. The Lorde
so and so to me, yf ought then death only
departe the and me asondre.

When she saw ↄ she was stedfastly myn-
ded to go wyth her, she lefte speakyng vnto
her. And so they went both, vntyll they came to Bethlehem. And when they were come to Bethlehem, it was noysed of thē throw all the cytie, and the wemē sayd: is not
this Naomi? And she answered thē: call me
not Naomi✱ (that is to saye, bewtifull) but call me
Mara, ✱ (that is to saye, bitter.) for ↄ Allmighty
hath made me verye bitter. I went out full,
and ↄ Lorde hath brought me home agayne
emptie. Why then call ye me Naomi: seing
Lorde hath humbled me, and the allmighty
hath brought me vnto aduersyte? And

sayde vnto him: wilt thou haue ȝ̄ seuen yeres hunger to come in thy lande, oꝛ wilt ȝ̄ flee.iij. monethes before thyne enemyes, they folowing the, oꝛ that there be thre dayes pestilence in thy land? Now therfore aduyse ȝ̄, ȝ se, what answere I shall geue to hym that sent me. And Dauid sayde vnto Gad: I am in extreme trouble. ⁎ We will fall now into the hande of the Loꝛde, foꝛ moch is his mercye, ād lett me not falle into ȝ̄ hand of man.

And so ȝ̄ Loꝛd sent a pestilence in Israel. frō the moꝛnyng vnto the tyme appoynted. And there dyed of the people from Dan to Beerseba seuenty thousand men. And when the Angell stretched out hys hand vpon Jerusalem to destroye it, the Loꝛde had compassion to do that euell, and sayd to the Angell that destroyed the people: it is now sufficient: holde thyne hande. And the Angell was by ȝ̄ threschyng place of Aresna the Jebusite. And Dauid spake vnto ȝ̄ Loꝛd (whē he saw the Angell that smote the people) ād sayde: loo, it is I that haue synned, and I that haue done wyckedly. But these shepe, what haue they done? lett thyne hande (I praye the) be agaynst me and agaynst my fathers house.

And Gad came the same daye to Dauid, and sayde vnto him: go vp and reare an aultare vnto the Loꝛd in the threschyng flowꝛe of Aresna the Jebusite. And Dauid (accoꝛdyng to the sayng of Gad) went vp, as the Loꝛde commaunded. And Aresna loked, ād saw the kyng and hys seruauntes comyng toward him. And Aresna wēt out, and bowed him selfe before the kyng flat on his face vpon the ground, and Aresna sayd: wherfoꝛe is my Loꝛde the kyng come to hys seruaūt? Dauid āswered: to bye the threschyng flowꝛe of the, and to make an aultare vnto the Loꝛde, that the plage maye cease from the people.

And Aresna sayde vnto Dauid: let my Loꝛde the kyng take and offer what semyth hym good in his eyes: Beholde, here be oxen foꝛ burnt sacrifice, and sleades and the other instrumentes of the oxen foꝛ wood. All these thynges dyd Aresna geue vnto the kyng, and sayd moꝛeouer vnto the kyng: the Loꝛd

¶ The thirde boke of

the Kynges after the rekenyng of the Latenistes: which thirde boke and the fourth also, is but one with the Hebꝛues.

¶ The fyꝛst Chapter.

¶ The young virgin Abisag kepeth Dauid in his extreme age. Adonia occupieth the reaulme vnwittyng to his father. Salomon is annoynted kyng, and so Adonia getteth him awaye.

And king Dauid was olde ȝ stryken in yeres: so that whā they couered hym wt clothes, he caught no heate. Wherfoꝛe hys seruauntes sayd vnto hym: let there be sought foꝛ my Loꝛde ȝ̄ kyng a youg mayden, to stonde before the kyng and to cheryshe hym. And let her lye in thy bosome, ȝ̄ my Loꝛd ȝ̄ king maye get heate. And so they sought foꝛ a fayꝛe damosell thoꝛow out all ȝ̄ coastes of Israel, ȝ found one Abisag a Sunamite, ȝ bꝛought her to the kyng. And the damosell was excedyng fayꝛe, ād cherisshed the kyng, ȝ ministred to him: But the kyng knew her not.

And Adonia the sonne of Hagith exalted him self, saying: I wilbe kyng. And he gatt him charettes ȝ hoꝛsmen, and fyftie men to runne before him. And his father wolde not displease him at anye time, noꝛ sayd so moch

A Jewel of Persian Literature

Nizami Ganjavi, *Khamsah*, 1540. St John's College MS Browne 1434

Shiraz, Benares, Calcutta, Tellicherry, Deptford, London, St John's College. These are the travels – as far as we can reconstruct them – of the manuscript that is undoubtedly the jewel of the Library's South and West Asian Collections.

MS Browne 1434 is a copy of one of the best known Persian classics, the *Khamsah* (*Quintet*) of the twelfth-century central Asian poet Jamal ud-Din Nizami Ganjavi. The *Khamsah* is a compendium of five long poems: the mystical *Makhzan al-asrar* ('Treasure of mysteries'); a biography of Alexander the Great, the *Iskandar namah* ('The book of Alexander'); and three romances, *Laila o Majnun* ('Laila and the possessed lover'), *Khusrau o Shirin* ('Khusrau and Shirin') and *Haft paykar* ('The seven beauties').

The St John's *Khamsah* was completed in Safar AH 947 / June 1540 CE. The text's colophon once recorded the names of its scribe and patron, but these (and a number of owners' seals) have subsequently been effaced by one or more of the dealers or brokers who moved the manuscript through India. Because the text's thirty fine illustrations are in the style of the school of Shiraz (in present-day Iran), we can assume that its ultimate origins are in or near that town.

Like many other fine manuscripts of the Persian classics copied or illustrated in Iran – and indeed like many Iranian poets, mystics and adventurers – the manuscript was drawn inexorably toward India as the wealth and power of the Great Mughals increased during the seventeenth century. A notation on the opening flyleaf indicates that the manuscript made its way into an as yet unidentified Indian library in 1740 through the agency of a Hindu broker.

The subsequent fate of the St John's *Khamsah* is a history of eighteenth-century India in microcosm. The manuscript appears to have been removed from the princely library of Benares after the British East India Company's victory over the Mughals at Buxar in 1764. From there it was taken to the Company's new town of Calcutta, where it would have found an eager market: native bureaucrats wrote and kept records in Persian, and interested Company officials studied Indian texts and languages in their leisure time. Bombay merchant Richard Bate bought the *Khamsah* against the objections of local Muslims. He eventually stripped it of its binding to ship it more cheaply from the South Indian town of Tellicherry to his father James, rector of St Paul's Church in Deptford and a former Fellow at St John's. James Bate's second son encased the *Khamsah* in a binding decorated in the chinoiserie style popular at the time, rich with pagodas and palanquin processions.

The letter of donation to the College in 1770 contains one final intriguing detail. James Bate learned that an educated Indian named Ghun Siam Das (Ghanshyamdas) was visiting London from Delhi. Bate took the manuscript to London, and the Indian visitor identified its contents and date. His mention of Ghanshyamdas is one of only a small handful of references to educated Indian visitors to Britain before the 1780s.

The manuscript's travels are therefore an apt depiction of the final flowering of the transnational Persian literary culture. This world, soon to pass away in favour of local languages and the rising global prestige of English, stretched from Istanbul to Java at the time the *Khamsah* was copied; by the time the manuscript found its way to the College, it had come to include for a brief moment the English in India and in England.

Jeevan Deol

Opposite: Shirin visiting Farhad on Mount Bisitun, where the latter is digging a canal, p. 160.

بدستش آهن از دل کرمزشید	بدنش نیلگری کند برنگل	بدتنی سنگ از دل برمیرشید	آبمن سنگ از گل بنرمیرشید
بدتش واکردند بریادومن	شکرلب باس باخودو ساغری بسر	خوبو بوش حراتب میترآشید	دلش راعشق آن بت نیت میخا

بنه شیر ازبرباشد هم شود نوش	چوشیرین یاقتی شده م آکبش	بشرینی چکوبم چون شکرخورد	تنه شهر آنکه شبرین جوامد
مزودترسب ازکوکمرکشین	شه را مش گران ازتن کشید	زمجلس غم زتن کرد قا	خو غاشق مشکتت ازخامتی

Left to right: A mounted battle between Khosrow and Bahram Chubina,
p. 129; Layla and her companions in a palm tree grove, p. 285; Alexander the
Great's battle with the Russians, p. 655; Alexander the Great enjoying outdoor
entertainment, p. 671.

A Bureaucrat with a Poet's Heart

Thomas Sackville, *The Complaint of Henry, Duke of Buckingham, c.* 1560. St John's College MS L.7

Introducing her 1936 edition of this important manuscript, Marguerite Hearsey argues that at the end of his life Thomas Sackville (*c.* 1536–1608) retained 'the heart of a poet'. The argument probably has to be made, as Sackville's career was political rather than literary. Baron Buckhurst, Earl of Dorset, and Lord Treasurer under James I, he died a bureaucrat's death, apparently succumbing to a stroke while sitting at the Privy Council table in 1608. Sackville seems to have followed convention: as Michael Schmidt has it, he 'wrote verse early and fell silent in later life … Lyric poetry was a young man's art.'

The *Complaint*, a contribution to the second part of the collaborative *Mirror for Magistrates* (1563), describes a descent into hell and consequent encounters with emblematic and historical figures, including Henry Stafford, Duke of Buckingham, first an ally and then an enemy and victim of Richard III. Like its companion texts, this highly regarded poem aims to teach good conduct by way of negative example. After the long poem's conclusion, the manuscript – of unknown provenance, and the object of some weak speculation that Sackville was a Johnian – offers an unfinished epilogue, many of its stanzas incomplete. The emotional register of this unfinished portion is consistent with the melancholia that has gone before, but of particular note is the explicit engagement with the art to which Sackville has turned his hand.

Across several stanzas the speaker suggests that neither Virgil nor Chaucer would be up to the task of expressing 'my sorowes nor my feares'. The combination of expressed humility and implicit arrogance is compelling: on one hand Sackville professes to 'crave pardon' rather than 'praise', and yet for somebody who considers his own versifying insufficient he does not show many signs of modest restraint, devoting many words to decrying the weakness of those very words. He even incorporates the writing of his predecessors: he borrows language from a poem falsely attributed to Chaucer when he refers to 'the pen wherewith he wrote the pain | of woful mary woful magdalain'; and he partakes in a tradition of self-deprecation when he writes, as the stanzaic regularity begins to break down,

> mine eloquence is rudeness
> I have no fresh licour out of the conduictes of Calliope.
> I haue no flowers of rethoricke through Clio.

And the manuscript has something even better in store. One couplet declares 'I am to rude to boistous is my stile | unsmoth and raggd more rougher than the file', a neat critique made more appealing by the flurry of corrections on its second line:

> I am to rude to boistous is my stile
> unsmoth and ragged and unsmoth more rougher
> than the file.

It is fair, in the context, to suggest that the deletions are the result of Sackville perceiving a compositional, rather than a transcriptional, error. One can but speculate as to specific thought processes, but it is worth noting especially the decision to call the style 'raggd' rather than 'ragged', and worth considering that, to modern ears anyway, 'raggd more rougher' is less smooth than 'ragged rougher'. This description of badness is not at all bad, or not unselfconsciously so. Those who concur with Schmidt's description of Sackville's verse as 'verbose', 'laboured' and 'mechanical' will find it particularly instructive to see the labour behind the verbal mechanism, the place where the poet's heart beat in secret.

Adam Crothers

Opposite and above: Details from fos 8v and 26r.

The Queen's Command

Signet letter of Elizabeth I commanding the election of Richard Cox, son of the late Bishop of Ely, to an Ely Fellowship, 29 May 1585. St John's College Archives D94.398

The imposition of Henry VIII's statutes in 1545, the restoration of Bishop John Fisher's statutes under the Catholic regime of Mary I in 1553, and the granting of a fresh code of College regulations under the Protestant regime of Elizabeth I in 1580, placed St John's directly in the sphere of Government influence, caught up in the political and religious changes of Tudor England. In this post-Reformation era of divided religious loyalties, a closer watch was kept to bind the College to the establishment. Masters of Colleges were given greater authority, and were frequently chosen or approved by Elizabeth and her ministers. Occasionally the Crown, exercising its role as patron along with private benefactors, also interested itself in the election of particular Fellows. Letters from private patrons and would-be patrons survive in the correspondence of College Masters, while those from the Crown are found as copies in the College Archives and also in the Docket Books at the National Archives.

The letter illustrated here, sent by Elizabeth to St John's College under the authority of the queen's signet seal, is of particular interest because it illustrates the leverage of the Crown arising from its control of vacant bishoprics. The bishops of Ely had been patrons of the Hospital of St John which Lady Margaret Beaufort had transformed into the College seventy years earlier, and from this ancient patronage stemmed their right, which endured until 1860, to nominate the holder of one of the College's Fellowships. In late May 1585, however, the see of Ely was vacant. The bishop had died and pending an appointment of his successor the right of nomination to these College Fellowships had lapsed to the Crown. Deliberately taking her time over the choice of a new bishop, Elizabeth accordingly exercised her right of patronage in favour of Richard Cox, the son and namesake of the late bishop. Cox was originally a member of Jesus College, but had, it seems, 'migrated' to St John's, and it was from here that he had taken his BA degree in 1583. Royal goodwill counted for a lot in those days. It gave the young man a fine start in life, which personal ability and family connections seem to have exploited. The *Dictionary of National Biography* tells us that he became a person 'of some influence in the Isle of Ely'.

Malcolm Underwood

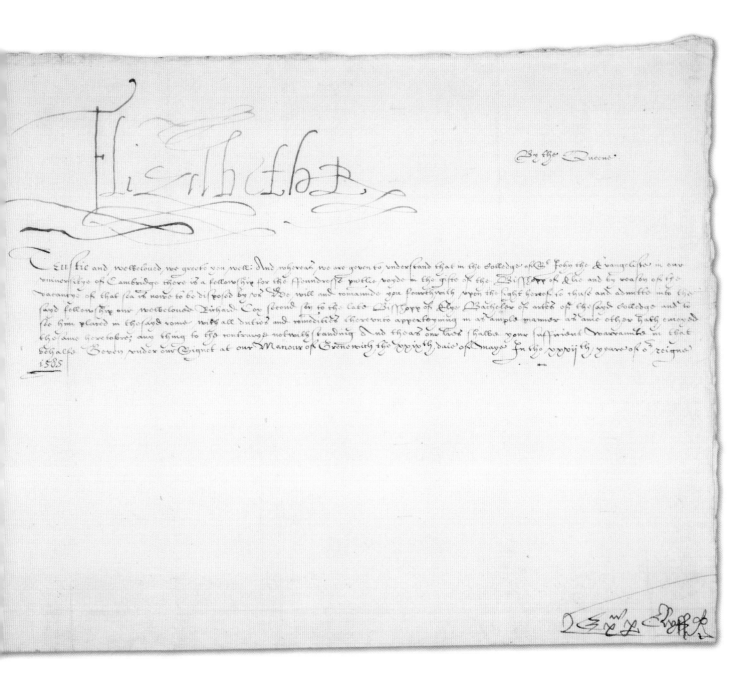

Elizabeth R.

By the Queene.

Trustie and welbeloued we greete you well. And whereas we are geuen to vnderstand that in the Colledge of St John the Euangeliste in our Vniuersitye of Cambridge there is a fellowshipp for the ffoundresse publiq voyde in the gifte of the Bisshopp of Elie and by reason off the vacancye off that sea is nowe to be disposed by vs: We will and comaunde you fourthwith vpon the sight hereof to chuse and admitte into the sayd fellowshipp our welbeloued Richard Coy second son to the late Bisshopp off Elye Bacheler of artes off the sayd Colledge and to see him placed in the sayd rome with all duties and comodities thereunto apperteyning in as ample manner as anie other hath enioyed the same heretofore: any thing to the contrarye notwithstanding. And these our Ires shalbe your sufficient warrantes in that behalfe. Geuen vnder our Signet at our Manour off Grenewich the xxixth daie off Maye In the xxviith yeare off o' reigne 1585

'Petty Emotions' with Public Significance

Sir Philip Sidney, *The Countess of Pembroke's Arcadia*, before 1588. St John's College MS I.7

The great Elizabethan courtier poet Sir Philip Sidney (1554–86) breaks up his *Old Arcadia* – a prose romance involving nobility, shepherds, pseudonyms, cross-dressing, infidelity, murder and similarly compelling matter – with a series of pastoral poems or 'eclogues', in which characters sing of love sought and lost. Among the eclogues' poetic distinctions is the introduction into English of the sestina, a verse form involving the repetition of six key words at the line ends. Sidney even offers a double sestina, and a rhyming one; but the one sestina that would now be considered conventional is incorporated into the body of the narrative as a song of mourning in the fourth book, rather than included in an eclogue.

This might seem, and might even be, a trivial distinction. But the dynamics of the *Old Arcadia*'s formal structure and those of the social arrangement in it are conceivably mutually informative phenomena. Indeed, one would do well to consider first the publication history of the text, starting with the nature of the dedication to the author's sister Mary, Countess of Pembroke. Sidney (whose godfather was Philip II, and whose mother had the dubious honour of catching smallpox from Elizabeth I) stresses the private nature of the composition: 'a trifle, and that triflingly handled', 'fitter to be swept away than worn to any other purpose', it is written 'only for you' and not for 'severer eyes'. He would revise it as the (unfinished) *New Arcadia*, and the *Old*, which survives in several manuscript copies but not in the author's hand, would not be widely published until the twentieth century. The Library's impressive manuscript, donated in the eighteenth century by the antiquarian Thomas Baker, is considered one of the most accurate and hence most important, and was the basis of Jean Robertson's 1973 edition.

While the plot is fuelled by the apparently petty emotions of individuals, the political stature of the figures – Duke Basilius, for instance, and two disguised princes – grants their private concerns public significance. Not without reference to the main narrative, the eclogues reinvent its world as one in which individual self-expression might favour rather than corrupt an ideal social order: the shepherds' songs allow love, for example, to be abstracted away from the specifics of extra-marital lust, deception or rape. As such, the sestina embedded in the fourth book can be understood as a focal point for the public/private tensions of the story, the form and the text.

That 'public' is among the sestina's repeating key words suggests some authorial awareness of such a duality. Admiring Sidney's sestinas, the distinguished literary critic William Empson speculates that 'the capacity even to conceive so large a form as a unit of sustained feeling, is one that has been lost since that age': whether or not this is true, it is striking that the fourth book's sestina manages to place so much emotional weight upon the word 'public', lamenting that

> …*our mischief grows in this vile fortune,*
> *That private pangs cannot breathe out in public*
> *The furious inward griefs with hellish wailing…*

Sidney claims to have sent sheets of the *Old Arcadia* to his sister 'as fast as they were done'. However modest his stated ambitions for the work, he clearly wished to 'breathe out' something 'inward', and not to keep it wholly private.

Adam Crothers

Opposite: The first folio of the manuscript, with ownership inscriptions.

Will Bodker of Chesmick in Middlesex
bought this Booke among other Manuscripts
of the Executor
of Sr Edmonde
Scorie Knight
And now possesses it
A D 1633

The first Booke or Acte of the
Countesse of Pembrokes Arcadia

Arcadia amonge all the Provinces of Grece was ever had
in singuler reputacion, partely for the sweetnes of the ayre
and other naturall benefittes, but principally for the moderate
and well tempered myndes of the people, who fynding how
true a contentacion is gotten by folowing the course of Nature
and how the shyning title of glory so much affected by other
Nacions, dothe in deede helpe litle to the happines of lyfe, were
the only people which as by theyr Justice and providence
gave neyther cause nor hope to theyr neighboures to annoy them,
so were they not stirred wth false prayse to trouble others
quyet, thinking it a small reward for the wasting of theyr
owne lyves in ravening; that theyr Posterity should long
after saye they had done so. Even the Muses seemed to
approve theyr good determynacion by choosing that Countrey
as theyr chiefest reposing place, and by bestowing theyr
perfections so largely there, that the very shepeherdes have theyr
fancyes lyfted to so high conceiptes, as the
learnedest of other nacions have bene long tyme since content
both to borrowe theyr names and imitate theyr Cunning. In this
place some tyme there dwelled a mighty Duke named Basilius
a Prince of sufficient skill to governe so quyet a Countrey,
where the good myndes of the former princes had sett downe
good lawes, and the well bringing up of the people, dyd
serve as a most sure bande to keepe them. He marryed Gynecia
the daughter of the king of Cyprus, a Lady worthy
enough to have had her name in recorde in all remembrance
if her latter tyme had not blotted her well governed
youthe; although the wounde fell more to her owne conscience
then to the knowledge of the world, fortune something
supplying her wante of vertue. Of her the Duke had two
faire daughters the elder Pamela the younger Philoclea
bothe so excellent in all those giftes which are allotted to
reasonable creatures, as they seemed to be borne for a sufficient
proof that nature is no stepmother to that sex, how
much soever the rugged disposicion of some men, sharpe
witted only in evill speaking hath sought to disgrace them.
And these two were brought up in such good manner till Pamela
was about ... then, Philoclea came to the point of seventeen
yeres of age. At which tyme the Duke Basilius, not so
much stirred wth the care for his Countrey and children, as
wth the vanity which possesseth many, who making a
perpetuall mansion of this poore bayting place of mans
lyfe, are desyrous to knowe the certenty of thinges to
come, wherein there is nothing so certen as our continuall uncerteynty,
Basilius, I saye, would needes undertake a Jorney to Delphos
there by the Oracle to enforme hym self, whether the rest
of his lyfe should be continued in like tenor of happines

Tho: Baker Coll: Jo: Socius Ejectus

Liber olim Dnahis: Viri Thome Wagstaff.

Swimming Against the Tide

Everard Digby, *De arte natandi*, 1587. St John's College Aa.6.19

Life in St John's during the latter part of the sixteenth century was far from easy and anything but comfortable. Amid the cold winters of England's 'Little Ice Age', students and Fellows alike were part of a rigorous, Calvinist foundation, presided over by a strict Master, William Whitaker. Whitaker suspected – possibly with good reason – that some senior figures among the Fellowship harboured Roman Catholic sympathies. Many men and women in late Elizabethan England concealed support for the 'old' religion behind a superficial show of conformity to the new Anglican Church. High on his list of suspects was Everard Digby, the Rector of Glaston, Rutland, and the author of *Theoria analytica*, an ambitious compendium of knowledge and a scheme for research based on the ancient philosophers and recent Continental authorities including Jacques Charpentier.

The quarrel between Whitaker and Digby became public in 1587, when the Master accused his colleague of having attacked Calvinists and having concentrated in his preaching on angels and other 'popish' subject matter. He tried to eject Digby from his Fellowship but Digby, evidently a robust man with strong principles, was unwilling to go quietly. Both parties called on powerful allies: Digby on the most powerful Johnian of them all – William Cecil, Lord Burghley, Lord Treasurer of England; Whitaker on Elizabeth I's long-time favourite the Earl of Leicester. After some months of strife, which drew attention to wider disputes in St John's at that time, Digby left his Fellowship. It is not clear whether the departure was voluntary; certainly it had become inevitable.

Among his other charges, Whitaker accused Digby of conduct unbecoming a Fellow of St John's: of being excessively noisy and coarse, far too preoccupied by outdoor exercise. He had recent evidence on which to base the charge, for in 1587 Digby published *De arte natandi*, a Latin work on swimming. Indeed it is tempting to suggest that publication on so frivolous a subject was for Whitaker the final straw. Not that *De arte natandi* seems particularly frivolous today. The historian of British swimming, Nicholas Orme, notes that the book combined a philosophical argument for a popular pastime with helpful advice on particular strokes. Illustrated with delightful woodcuts, showing swimmers disrobing on grassy riverbanks watched over by cattle before striking out naked into a swiftly flowing stream, the second part of *De arte natandi* is a practical manual, perhaps the first of its kind in western Europe. It proved extremely influential: Christopher Middleton's accessible 1595 English abridgement of Digby's work, *A Short Introduction for to Learne to Swimme*, sold well, while the strictures of Digby and Middleton were in time taken up by seventeenth-century authors such as Melchisédech Thévenot, whose seminal *L'Art de nager* was published in Paris in 1696.

Digby died in 1605. Confusingly, a namesake and cousin was involved in the Gunpowder Plot that same year, and was executed in London late in January 1606.

Mark Nicholls

Opposite: One of the illustrative woodcuts, slightly enlarged.

In the Language of the People

Y Beibl Cyssegr-lan: sef yr Hen Destament, a'r Newydd, translated by William Morgan, 1588.
St John's College A.4.15★

St David's Day in the College Chapel is rather special. The readings are unfamiliar to many in the congregation, but for the Welsh speakers present they have a powerful and poetic resonance. The eagle lectern bears a modest volume: *Y Beibl* of William Morgan, published in 1588.

Simple rubrication on the title page is the work's sole decoration. Plainly printed, without illustrations or fine initials, the beauty of this Bible lies in its language. Central to the Protestant Reformation was the conviction that every man and woman should be able to understand the Word of God for himself or herself without need for a mediator. Luther himself translated the Bible into German. The dangers faced by the early translators and printers of the Bible in English are well known, ending only with Henry VIII's plan to place a copy of his Great Bible in every parish in the land (see p. 88). Both Henry and Edward VI ordered that lessons in services should be read in English throughout England and Wales. But for a sizeable minority of the population English was not their native tongue, and the readings made no more sense than Latin.

The first attempt to produce a Welsh Bible saw the publication of William Salesbury's translation of the New Testament in 1567. Incomplete, and criticised for archaic and cumbersome language, this failed to meet the need for a translation that spoke directly to all Welsh worshippers. Responsibility for a Welsh Bible passed to William Morgan (1545–1604), in later life Bishop first of Llandaff and later of St Asaph. A tenant farmer's son from Penmachno, Caernarvonshire, Morgan probably received his early education through the house of Gwydir, renowned for their Welsh bardic patronage. He entered St John's College as a sub-sizar, performing menial duties in return for his keep, and here studied Greek and Hebrew under some of the finest scholars of the age. His linguistic abilities, combined with a deep-rooted love of Welsh literary tradition and language, fitted him for the task of translation. Convinced that his parishioners should have access to the Scriptures in their own tongue, he began his biblical translation independently whilst a poor parish priest at Llanrhaeadr, reliant on Cambridge friends for books and advice. He later admitted despairing of completing more than the Pentateuch, the first five books of the Old Testament. Recognising the quality of his work the Archbishop of Canterbury, John Whitgift, persuaded him to continue, and, on completion of his translation in 1587, urged him to expedite its printing. The established Church had been strongly censured by the Welsh Puritan John Penry for its failure to provide a Welsh Bible, and with a real and imminent threat of a Spanish invasion there was urgent need to strengthen the Protestant cause in Wales, where Spain might find support.

Morgan's Bible was printed by the deputies of the Queen's Printer, Christopher Barker, and copies were ordered to be placed in every Welsh-speaking parish by Christmas 1588. It was greeted rapturously by contemporary poets and churchmen alike. Besides its enduring legacy in cementing the Protestant Reformation in Wales, the language of Morgan's Bible set a standard for generations of Welsh poets and prose writers.

Kathryn McKee

Y BEIBL CYS-SEGR-LAN. SEF YR HEN DESTA-MENT, A'R NEWYDD.

2. Timoth. 3. 14, 15.

Eithr aros di yn y pethau a ddyſcaiſt, ac a ymddyried-
wydi ti, gan wybod gan bwy y dyſcaiſt.
Ac i ti er yn fachgen wybod yr ſcrythur lân, yr hon
ſydd abl i'th wneuthur yn ddoeth i iechydwria-
eth, trwy'r ffydd yr hon ſydd yng-Hriſt Ieſu.

Imprinted at London by the Deputies of
CHRISTOPHER BARKER,
Printer to the Queenes moſt excel-
lent Maieſtie.

1588.

'God Blew and They Were Scattered'

Robert Adams, *Expeditionis Hispanorum in Angliam vera descriptio*, 1590. St John's College Aa.5.5

The defeat of the Spanish Armada in the summer of 1588 left many people in England as puzzled as they were relieved. The precise intentions of the Spanish fleet had been obscure, and the mix of tactics and good fortune which brought victory were known only to a few. There was thus a market for further information on these dramatic events.

Published in 1590, this handsome volume of engraved plates, a separate issue of the maps to Petruccio Ubaldini's *A Discourse concerning the Spanishe Fleete*, sets out to provide essential details in an attractive, visual manner, combining propaganda and elegance in equal measure. The maps convey King Philip of Spain's muddled strategy: the advance of a great fleet eastwards along the English Channel, from the first sighting of land off Cornwall to the attempted rendezvous with the Spanish Army of Flanders waiting to embark near Dunkirk, and on thereafter to the English use of fire-ships to break up the Armada's strong defensive formation and the subsequent haphazard fight off Gravelines and into the North Sea. Seaborne operations before the age of steam were always vulnerable to unexpected tricks

of wind and tide, and at this final stage in the battle, as the maps make a point of showing, the wind blew constantly from the south-west, frustrating Spanish attempts to regroup and obliging them to head home 'north about'. This led to many further casualties as ship after ship was wrecked and plundered on the Scottish and Irish coasts.

Bound in contemporary vellum, this copy is hand-coloured with energy and élan. The gunfire between the fleets is picked out in red, flags and pennants are given due detail, the cartouches and wind roses are multi-coloured, while a mass of darkness consistently emphasises the Armada's threatening 'wooden walls' as it moved slowly up the Channel. In commercial and artistic terms, and indeed when considered as propaganda, the maps drawn by the architect Robert Adams and engraved by Augustine Ryther were highly successful: today Adams' images of the crescent-shaped Armada are reproduced time and again in books, magazines and TV programmes, while the final, larger map of the British Isles, with the circular course of the Spanish fleet marked out clearly, emphasises the futility of the expedition. Ironically, this book appeared shortly after England, determined on an effective counter-thrust, tried to attack the Spanish and Portuguese coasts with an armada of its own, again with disastrous results.

Robert Adams died in 1595. The longstanding recipient of a personal pension from Elizabeth I who – understandably – admired his talents, he held the post of Surveyor of the Royal Works during the last year of his life.

Mark Nicholls

Opposite and left: Details from Map 6. Overleaf: The naval engagement off Calais, Map 8.

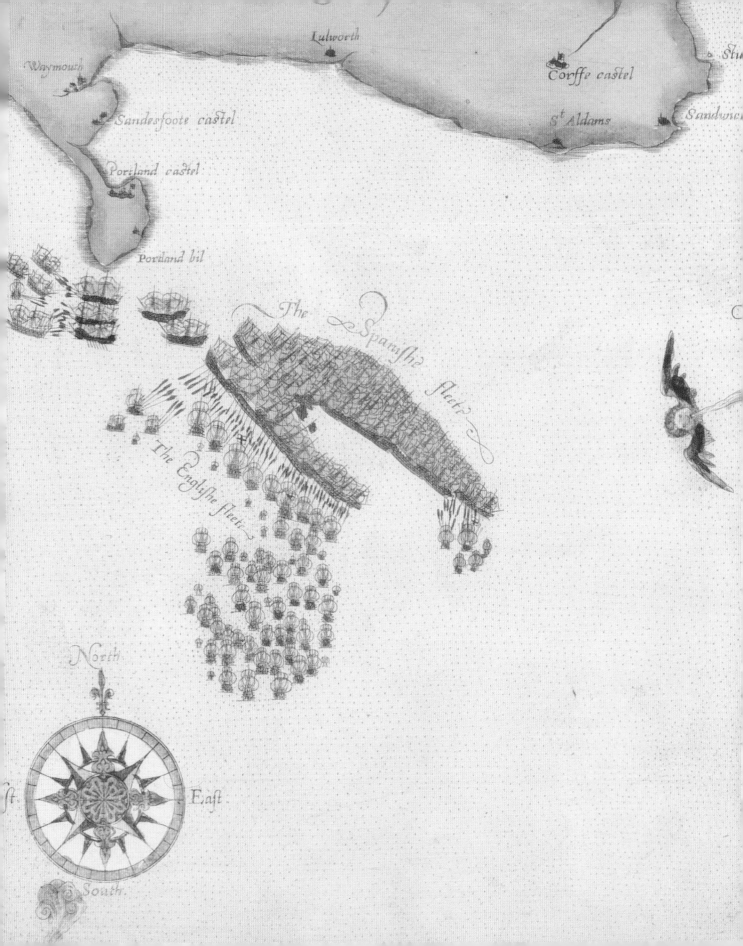

Waymouth

Lulworth

Corffe castel

Stu

Sandesfoote castel

St Aldams

Sandwic

Portland castel

Portland bil

The Spanyshe fleete

The Englyshe fleete

North

East

ft

South

PARTE   P·A·R·T·E   O·F

OF   S·V·S·S·E·X

HAMP.

SHIRE

Porchester   Havant

Chichester   Arondel   Bramber   Shoram   Brighthelmeston   Lewis   Pe

S.t borne

W·E·S·T

S.t Helens pointe   Owers

The Englishe fleete

HONI SOIT QVI MAL Y PENSE

The Scale of English miles   Roberto Adamo authore

PARTE OF

KENT

Sandwitch
Sandowne
Deale
Wawmore
South forlande

Wide
Doure

Aphledowre
Ramny

Rie
Lenit

Winchelsey
Dunge nesse
Hastinge
Faire lee

The English fleete

The Spanishe fleete

Cales
Calis cleeues

Blacke nesse

PART

Bolongne

OF

Estaples
Monstrell

Crotoye
Valeryt
Ashaualle

The Spanishe fleete

Treporte

Dipe

PICARDIE

SEMPER EADEM

The Lie of the Land

Map of the College's Thorrington Hall estate, Essex, 13 September 1618.
St John's College Archives MPS72

The manor of Thorrington (or Thorington) Hall, Essex, was granted to the College in 1521 with that of Ridgewell, about thirty miles to the north-west, by two of Lady Margaret's executors, John Fisher, Bishop of Rochester, and Hugh Ashton, Archdeacon of York. Thorrington is renowned for its more than 100 acres of woodland, and the fine timber grown there has been exploited systematically by the College since at least the late eighteenth century. Between 1788 and 1820 the wood from Thorrington realised between £300 and £500 annually, a significant sum at that time.

Thorrington Hall farm, an estate of some 600 acres, was generally prosperous and in 1816 the Senior Bursar noted that its 'main premises were good and in good repair – house in good repair and contains abundance of rooms and conveniences'. Bursars kept an eye on such things. Thorrington was one of the places in which the nineteenth-century College, mindful of its wider educational obligations, donated a site for a local school (in 1865).

This map is the earliest of a number of picturesque representations of Thorrington held in the College Archives, the others dating from the late eighteenth century, specifically between 1784 and 1797. Its detailed and engaging depiction of particular buildings illustrates the care devoted by St John's to lands scattered across England. Indeed it typified the well-managed agricultural estate that underpinned College finances through much of the history of St John's. While farming land cost money, time and labour to look after, it was long regarded as a prudent long-term investment for an institution that sought to sustain its prosperity across centuries rather than mere decades. College estates in Kent, Lincolnshire, Yorkshire, Cambridgeshire and Essex, with smaller holdings elsewhere, stretched across more than 15,000 acres in the twentieth century.

Malcolm Underwood

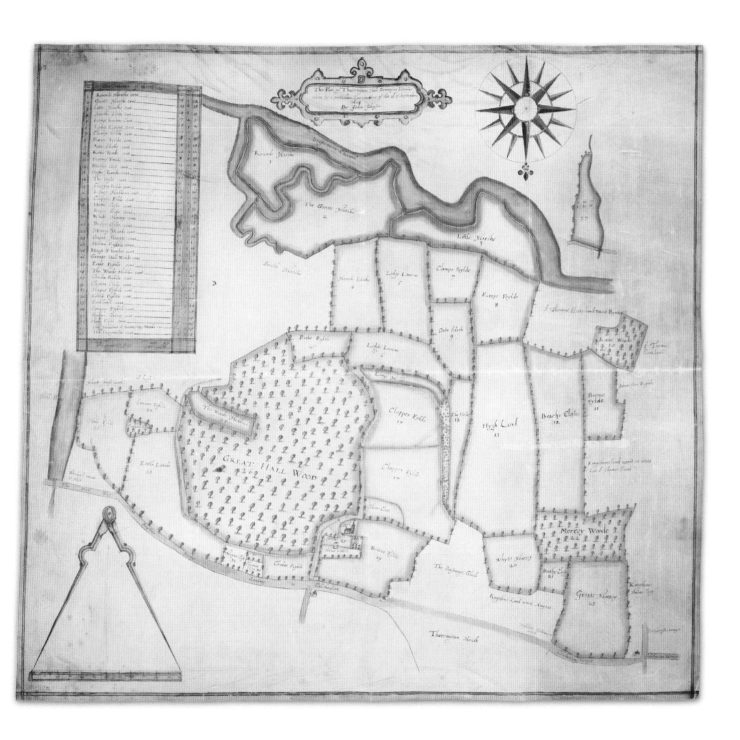

The World in your Pocket

John Seller, *Atlas maritimus*, 1682. St John's College F.12.21

Seller by name and seller by profession, but John Seller was more than that. Styled 'Hydrographer to the King's Most Excellent Majestie' (Charles II), he was a leading London maker of maps and charts and a dealer in navigational instruments. These he made and sold from his premises in the Royal Exchange and Hermitage Stairs in Wapping. At Thames-side he could both sell to sea captains and gain from them new observations and information to add to his charts.

In the early seventeenth century, map- and chart-making was still firmly in the hands of the Dutch, and for his first charts Seller was dependent upon their expertise even to the extent of buying their old copper plates and re-engraving parts of them to make them his own. Relying heavily on Dutch knowledge, he compiled and published *The English Pilot* in 1671 and, in 1675, his *Atlas maritimus*. The contents of both concentrate upon navigation of the seas around Britain and on the expanding interests of the English overseas, particularly along the seaboard of North America and the Caribbean.

Seller's *Atlas maritimus* was a large volume consisting of some thirty maps and charts. While it might have been seen in his shop or in a ship's cabin, it certainly couldn't have been easily carried around. This may be the reason why he produced a pocket-sized version, of which we are fortunate to have a 1682 copy in the College Library, one of many seventeenth-century books presented to St John's by a Master of the College, Humphrey Gower. It is an exquisite hand-coloured item, which, as the title page proclaims, describes 'the Sea Coasts Capes Headlands Bayes Roads Harbors and Ports in most of the known parts of the World'.

After fourteen pages of text which briefly describe the location of places, and provide an image of the mariner's compass, there follows a new map of the world according to Mercator, the leading map-maker of the day. It shows that while Europeans already had a good knowledge of Europe and of the outlines of the Americas and Africa, knowledge of the Far East was still only sketchy. There follow some detailed sea charts by John Seller (based largely on Dutch information) of the North Sea, the Thames estuary and the English Channel. Further afield there are charts of the Baltic, the coast of West Africa, and the eastern seaboard of North America. As well as charts, Seller included maps of the newly explored American mainland – Newfoundland, New England, New Jersey, Virginia, Maryland and the Carolinas – and there is a particularly good series of maps of the Bermudas and the Caribbean islands of Jamaica, Tobago and Barbados. These are among the most detailed maps in the volume, with many features and place-names included. Reflecting the island's importance to mariners in the South Atlantic, there is also a fascinating map of St Helena, on which are marked various lemon gardens, Orange Tree Valley, Tobacco Valley and the James Fort.

This beautiful pocket-size edition of the *Atlas maritimus* gives a remarkable insight into the world as it was then known to the English. Some parts of the Far East were still not known, even to the Dutch, and there are merely hints on the charts of Nova Zealandia, Hollandia Nova and Australia Incognita, gaps in maps which would only be filled over a century later.

Robin Glasscock

Opposite: Advertisement facing the title page, considerably enlarged, as is the map of St Helena overleaf.

All Sorts of
Instruments
belonging to
the art of
Navigation
are Sold by
John Seller

on the
Royall Exchange

in Long: from Pico Teneriffa: 13ᵈ - 50ᵐ

The Island of SAINT HELLENA.
By Iohn Seller.

Powells Bay
Sandy Point
Sandy Bay

Needles

Lott
Lotts Wife Valley

Horse feidge

Manate Bay

Lemon
Lemon Garden

Savana

rowds
Garden

OldLemon Garden

Man and
Horse point

Egg Island
Bird Island

Ledg of
Rocks

Pomp and Circumstance

Order of the English coronation service, seventeenth century. St John's College MS L.15

Even for those born since 1953, the image of families and neighbours crammed into optimistic front rooms to watch the new Elizabethan age dawn on tiny flickering screens is instantly familiar. Millions witnessed this centuries-old ritual redolent with symbolism. Tradition can reinforce legitimacy. Medieval kings, particularly those with questionable claims to the throne, traced the origin of their coronation rites to the crowning of the Anglo-Saxon King Edgar at Bath in 973. Tudor coronations followed the order in the *Liber regalis* of 1382. James I ordered the most obvious change, his coronation ceremony being translated into English.

Elements of the coronation date back centuries; even the anthem *Zadok the Priest* was sung long before Handel composed the setting familiar today. But the service, like the monarchy itself, has evolved and adapted to the circumstances of each age. This is illustrated strikingly by a unique document in St John's Library: MS L.15. This slim, unassuming volume, its neatly spaced text written in red and black in the clearest of hands, was – according to the note on page iii of the manuscript – the copy of the order of service Charles I himself held during his coronation. A snapshot of the ceremony in 1626, it was also the copy which Archbishop William Sancroft consulted when preparing the coronation of James II.

All English monarchs have been crowned in the context of a Holy Communion service. For James II this posed a serious problem. A convert to Roman Catholicism, he would not participate in Anglican communion, and ordered his Archbishop of Canterbury to abridge the lengthy coronation rites and remove the Eucharist.

Archbishop Sancroft was a Church of England loyalist. Conscious of the threat a Roman Catholic king posed to the Protestant establishment, he had tried unsuccessfully to persuade James back into the Anglican fold. A non-combatant but staunch royalist during the Civil War of the 1640s, he was devoted to the rule of law and opposed parliamentary factions trying to exclude a Catholic from the succession.

Sancroft's annotations to L.15, with its companion volume L.14 containing his final version of the service, are revealing. Historic prayers were dropped; the litany and *Veni Creator* moved. Ironically, producing a service acceptable to a Catholic made the English coronation service far more like Continental Protestant rites. Sancroft's annotations indicate more than simple abridgement. Wording was modernised throughout, 'thee' and 'thou' becoming 'you' in the final version. Where 'the Seale of Catholique faith' was bestowed, Sancroft wisely avoided ambiguity, changing 'Catholique' to 'Christian'. Changes went deeper, probably unintentionally. Despite Sancroft's personal absolute conviction of James's right to rule by birth, in the service that he and his bishops devised it was the established Church's bestowal of unction upon the king that accorded him divine authority, a subtle but historically significant constitutional change.

As an object, this manuscript has a direct personal link with Charles I. As a text, it illuminates a key moment in the changing relationship between Church, state and monarchy.

Kathryn McKee

Opposite: One of Sancroft's significant annotations. **Overleaf:** *The opening of the manuscript with note of its recovery from Westminster.*

shall sanctify may be holy, & whatso=
ever he shall blesse may be blessed. A=
men.

Then y^e ArchB^p putteth y^e Ring
on y^e fourth finger of y^e Kings right
hand saying:

Receive the Ring of Kingly
Dignity, & by it y^e Seale of Catho=
lique faith, y^t as this day thou art
adorned y^e Head & Prince of this
Kingdome & People, so thou maist
persevere as the Authour & Establish=
er of Christianity & the Christian
faith; y^t being rich in faith & happie
in workes thou maist reigne with him
that is King of Kings, to whome be.
honour & glory for ever & ever. Amen.

After the Ring is put on, y^e ArchB^p
saith this Prayer.

O God to whom belongeth all
power & dignity, give unto thy Servant
Charles

Recover'd frō Westmr. upon yᵉ Suit.

L. 15

This probably was the Book, which King Charles
the first held in his hand at his Coronation,
For wᶜʰ See ArchBp: Sancroft's note.

Blessed Kg Charles I. succeeding to the
Crown March 27th. 1625. consummated his
Marriage wth his Queen at Canterbury yᵉ Day
after Trinity-Sunday in yᵉ same year; but
was not crowned till Candlemass-Day after.
In yᵉ mean Time, it appears, yt he designd
to be crown'd together wth his Queen. For in yᵉ
intervall there was a Coronation-Office drawn
up both for King, & Queen; wch is still extant
in yᵉ King's paper-Office in Fol. large-paper.
But yᵉ Queen was not crown'd, for Reasons
easy to be conjectur'd. Whereupon (I conceive)
his Book was pᵖpar'd for yᵉ Crowning of the
King out of yᵉ former Draught, only leaving
out what concern'd yᵉ Queen. And I have
Reason to think, yt 'tis yᵉ very Book, wch the
King held in his Hand at yt great Solemnity.

But now oᵉ gracious Soveraim Ld. Kg James
being to be crown'd together wth the Queen;
I have wth my pen supplied yᵉ following Office,
& made it exactly agree wth yᵉ first Draught in
Ch. I's time, wch I had out of yᵉ paper-Office.
Elias Ashmole in his Collection of Coronation-Offices,
hath one (begining p. 301 r.) transscrib'd froᵐ yᵉ very MS.
wch Ch. yᵉ 2d us'd at yᵉ time of his Coronation. But it
is yᵉ same wth yt wch follows in this Book; only supplied
in some places out of what Dr Laud (who assisted at the
crowning of Ch. 1st as Vice-dean of Westmⁿ, being yⁿ also
Bp of S. Davids) added wth his own Hand in another Copie
of yt same Office (wch follows) abbridged, having only yᵉ
begining of yᵉ praiers, but yᵉ Rubrics entire, & very
pᵗticular; wch I suppose, he held in his own Hand yt Day,
for yᵉ Directio of sims. & yᵉ Kg. as his Duty was. /.

The Stuff of Medicine

William Heberden's Materia Medica Cabinet

This plain wooden cabinet, standing just over six feet tall, could be mistaken for a piece of domestic furniture. A small label in an eighteenth-century hand, 'Materia medica', gives a clue to the contents. Opening the drop-down front of the upper half reveals unexpected riches within: twenty-eight numbered drawers, increasing in depth from top to bottom. Each drawer is divided into compartments, containing samples catalogued under appropriate headings, mostly in Latin, with occasional comments in English: a treasure trove of the natural world from the exotic to the bizarre.

The specimens were assembled and housed in this cabinet by William Heberden, a physician and Fellow of St John's, who formed the collection to illustrate his series of lectures on materia medica, delivered annually from 1740 to 1748 in the Cambridge School of Anatomy. In his introductory lecture, Heberden helpfully defined his subject as 'all those natural substances which are either used themselves for the recovery of health, or from which any medicinal preparations are made'. The series of lectures – initially twenty-six but gradually increasing to thirty-one, with a break for the Newmarket races – was divided into four sections: Of Fossils, Of Vegetables, Of Animals and Of Chemicals. The cabinet's specimens are arranged similarly, with drawers for seeds; roots; flowers, nuts and fruit; woods; gums; barks; animal products; mineral products; and substances in stoppered bottles. The lower cupboard contains larger samples, including a 'Coco Nut' and a giant fungus.

Specimens came from near and far. Ginseng from North America and China, Peruvian bark from South America, and a small mummified skink (now known affectionately as 'the Library Lizard'), exact origin unknown, sit alongside samples gathered by Heberden himself. Alumina ore from Whitby and 'a substance found plentifully near the stinking well in

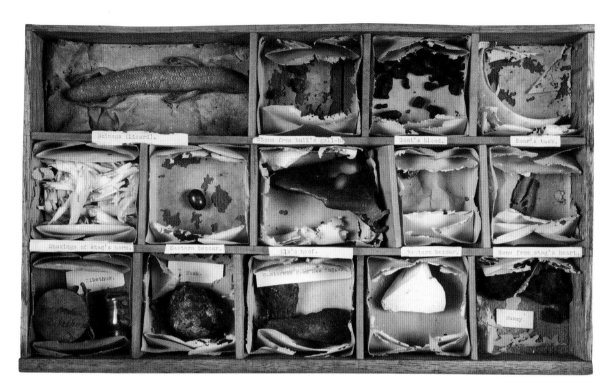

Harygate' were souvenirs of vacations in Yorkshire. Closer to home he collected a 'specimen from an old tree near the Abby of Bury St Edmund's' and 'a chalky substance from the water in Trinity College'.

While the contents of the materia medica cabinet may have been plentiful, the eighteenth-century physician had few reliable drugs available to him. Heberden's attitude to treatment was strikingly modern. He argued convincingly against mixing numerous potent ingredients, whose combined effects were unpredictable and potentially dangerous, persuading the Royal College of Physicians to

take a more robust view on traditional remedies. He also cautioned colleagues to resist assumptions that an individual patient's recovery could be attributed directly to a particular treatment, insisting that it was only 'facts repeated in a variety of circumstances that can establish the just reputation of a remedy'. His own meticulous case notes – later published – bear testament to a holistic and empirical approach, leading some to regard him as the father of modern medical practice.

The cornucopia of substances in Heberden's cabinet essentially formed a teaching aid to illustrate the history of medicine, not a practical pharmacy. Contemporary accounts describe his lectures as not just informative but entertaining. Only a man with a sense of humour would have labelled a small round pebble 'Philosopher's stone'.

Kathryn McKee

Opposite: A general view of the upper cabinet. Above: Specimens and bottles in Drawers 24 and 27.

Measuring Time and the World

Long-case regulator made by John Shelton, 1763

The 1760s were challenging and exciting times for the makers of highly accurate astronomical clocks or 'regulators', so-called because they were the clocks by which other timepieces could be set. Over forty years earlier, in 1716, the astronomer Edmond Halley had pointed out that on the rare occasions when Venus passes directly between the Earth and the Sun it would be possible with precise instrumentation to establish the distance of the Earth from the Sun, one of the fundamental units of astronomy. Halley, having regard to the unpredictability of weather and cloud cover, recommended that observations should be made from as many places as possible. Accurate pendulum clocks and the best available telescopes were essential.

John Shelton, a London clockmaker, rose to this challenge by producing five or six regulators (the number is uncertain) one of which is now in the College. One of the others went on Captain James Cook's voyage of 1768, promoted by the Royal Society to record the transit of Venus in 1769 from a favourable location in the South Pacific. Cook in addition had secret orders to explore unknown lands, and these orders resulted in the charting of the coast of New Zealand and the east coast of Australia. Charles Green, chief astronomer on Cook's ship the *Endeavour*, presumably set up the regulator on Tahiti before recording the transit there on 3 June 1769.

By that time 'our' regulator had been in the College for five years or so. It seems to have been presented to the College late in 1764 or early in 1765 by Richard Dunthorne, scientific assistant to Roger Long, Master of Pembroke College and Lowndean Professor of Astronomy and Geometry. It was held in a room in the College where 'a register of its going was constantly kept'. The mathematician William Ludlam noted that 'the clock of St John's College had been more regular than that at Greenwich'. In 1767, in anticipation of the transit of Venus, the clock was taken up and very carefully installed in the newly built observatory on the top of the Shrewsbury Tower in Second Court, where it was subsequently used by Ludlam, Adam Gooch and their successors in their astronomical observations and calculations.

Shelton's regulator is a beautifully crafted instrument; the train has a five-wheel, weight-driven movement of one month's duration, a dead-beat escapement with a thirty-tooth brass wheel and a gridiron temperature-compensated pendulum. On the square dial minutes are shown in the outer ring, seconds in the inner ring, and hours in the revolving

central volvelle. It is recorded that in the eighteenth century the clock's rate was accurate to within a second a day over a period of two years, a remarkable feat of timekeeping for the period and a tribute to the skills of its maker.

It is hard to imagine this beautiful instrument on the top of the Shrewsbury Tower, where it remained until the observatory was closed in 1859. It is uncertain where it was kept for the next hundred years, but, still in good order, it was loaned to the National Maritime Museum in 1966 and returned to the College in 1992. In its glazed mahogany case it may now be seen in the Exhibition Area between the Old and Working (New) Libraries.

Robin Glasscock

Defeating the Slave Trade

Letters and papers of Thomas Clarkson and William Wilberforce

There were many heroes of the campaign against the Atlantic slave trade, but unquestionably two of the greatest were members of St John's College: William Wilberforce and Thomas Clarkson, who matriculated in 1776 and 1779 respectively. Wilberforce, with his oratory and religious fervour, was effective in swaying opinion in Parliament and among the governing elite more generally. Clarkson, by contrast, might be regarded as the foot soldier of the campaign. He organised meetings, petitions, legal challenges and mass boycotts of rum and sugar, and he lobbied tirelessly behind the scenes and in

committees to keep the issue on the boil. His first big push was in 1787 when he dared to enter the lions' den of the slave trade, Bristol. His diary reveals his trepidation as he did so. 'The bells of some of the churches were then ringing; the sound filled me with a melancholy … I began now to tremble, for the first time, at the arduous task I had undertaken … I questioned whether I should even get out of it alive.'

Clarkson did get out, but when shortly afterwards he visited the other great slaving port of Liverpool he was attacked and almost drowned in the Mersey estuary. After that he went to Manchester, a town less dependent on the Atlantic and with no love for Liverpool, and suddenly Clarkson's campaign caught fire. A petition against the slave trade – apparently signed by 11,000 people, nearly one-fifth of the local population – is regarded by historians as the first mass petition on any subject. Manchester's enthusiasm in turn provoked competitive philanthropy in other cities and towns: 13,000 inhabitants of Glasgow, for example, petitioned in 1792. In place after place Clarkson seems to have been involved, writing thousands of letters to his contacts and riding about the country on horseback, covering 35,000 miles in seven hectic years.

Clarkson's campaigns have a historical significance beyond anti-slavery, in that about thirty per cent of his signatories in 1788, and only fifteen per cent in 1792, were members of what might be called the elite: nobles, corporators and freemen. This contrasts with the eighty to ninety per cent that was the norm for petitions in this period. As such they have been seen as the first stirring of a middle-class consciousness, the start of a long and halting process which ended in the 1830s when the business-owning middle classes established a hegemony in local government and a foothold in national politics. The anti-slavery crusade was also one of the first routes through which women began

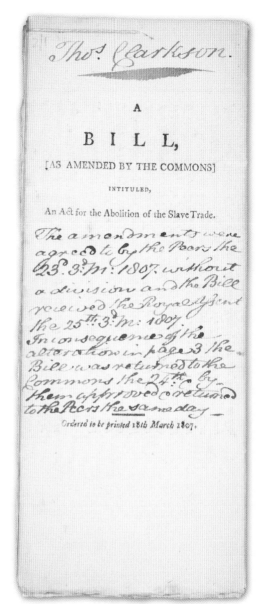

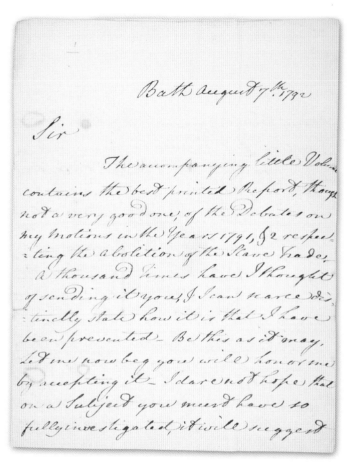

to be incorporated into civil society. Between 1790 and 1810 as many as ten per cent of subscriptions to the cause were in a female name, and women were also physically active in Clarkson's campaigns, especially the sugar boycotts.

Wilberforce was a politically conservative Anglican evangelical, whose hatred of slavery was linked to his sense of sin. A society grown rich on the suffering of the workers in the sugar plantations needed to propitiate the Almighty if it were to escape His vengeance. In that light, abolition of the slave trade – finally achieved in 1807 – would be an act of national atonement. Clarkson, by contrast, had radical

leanings and worked closely with Quaker abolitionists. He described himself as 'nine parts in ten of their way of thinking', and eventually gave up his Anglican orders. He worshipped a God of love, not vengeance. To him slavery was simply a hideous blot on creation.

Boyd Hilton

Above: Clarkson's personal copy of the 1807 Act and a letter from Wilberforce.
Left and overleaf: Clarkson's diary written in 1787.

this Hill, before I got to the Top & before I could see the Country below, there was no thing of Course to be seen beyond it but Clouds. These seemed to be continually rolling over the Top of the Hill like Smoke — I thought at first there was some ? below the Hill which I could not dis but that the Smoke was rising from the fire & blowing over the Hill so near were the Clouds to the Top — I think I never beheld so awful a Sight —

I observed that some Clouds moved faster than the others, and, when I expected those which went faster, at the time they appeared to come up with the slower to incorporated, they moved over them, so that universally the higher Clouds moved faster than the lower — The Country all about was hilly, and quite a Champain Country, without Trees — I breakfasted at Chippenham on Horseback at 10 o'Clock, arrived at Bath 13 miles at 12 o'Clock — I dined here. After dinner I walked

about ye Town and was much charmed
with it as well as with the Country about
it — I left the City at 6 oClock & arrived
at Bristol 12 miles on [foot] 8 — When I
came within a mile of this City, the weather
not being quite clear, it appeared to be very
bulky. the Bells of some of the Churches
were ringing at the Time. These with
the other Circumstance was productive
of some odd Sensations. I began rather
to tremble at the arduous Task of attemp
ting to subvert a Branch of ye Trade of ye
[City], and to encounter an Host of
[Peo]ple in it — However I became soon
calm and collected, and Seemed to gain
[fre]sh Spirits from my former Sensation
which only confirmed me the more, that
[I] must be doubly diligent, active, and
[per]severing in the Cause, which I had
undertaken — With these Resolutions I
entered the City, determining that no
Labour should appear too arduous, &
[it]s Treatment from the Inhabitants, should
[th]ey to know my Errand, be too horrid to

127

Changing the Face of English Poetry

William Wordsworth and Samuel Taylor Coleridge, *Lyrical Ballads, with a Few Other Poems*, 1798.
St John's College Wa 1798.1

Wordsworth to move to Bristol 'to superintend the printing'. Then something went wrong. It was probably money trouble again, Cottle's this time: by September 1798, although printing was complete and copies were circulating under Cottle's name, the volume was still not officially published. Cottle tried to sell the print run to the London publisher Thomas Longman; when that fell through, Wordsworth approached the radical publisher Joseph Johnson. Johnson had published both poets' work before and agreed to do so again now, so Wordsworth and Coleridge asked that the rights be transferred to him and then set sail for Germany. On 4 October 1798, however, newspapers announced the publication of 'Lyrical Ballads, with a few other

Wordsworth and Samuel Taylor Coleridge's joint publication, *Lyrical Ballads, with a Few Other Poems*, was described by Ernest Bernbaum as 'the most important poetical publication in the English language since the appearance of *Paradise Lost*'. But its first appearance in 1798, eleven years after Wordsworth had been admitted to St John's as an undergraduate, was fraught with complication. The pair first thought of writing something together in late 1797, when they had only been friends for a few months – primarily, as Wordsworth acknowledged, because their 'united funds were very small' and they wanted to go on holiday. 'Accordingly we set off', he continued, 'and in the course of this walk was planned the Poem of The Ancient Mariner', which grew until 'we began to talk of a volume'. This stalled briefly: both poets were working on other projects, including a play apiece and ambitious philosophical verse. But when the plays did not sell, and they realised that philosophical verse required a stay in Germany, work on the joint collection began in earnest – in order, as Coleridge told the Bristol publisher Joseph Cottle, 'to procure the money some other way'.

Having read both poets' work in manuscript, Cottle was sceptical about joint publication, particularly because Wordsworth and Coleridge wanted to remain anonymous. But in June 1798 matters seemed unambiguous enough for

This, the first Edition of the
Lyrical Ballads, consisted of
500 Copies and was published
by Cottle of Bristol, who in his "Remi-
niscences" informs us, "the sale was
so slow, and the severity of most of
the Reviews so great, that its progress
to oblivion seemed certain. I parted
with the largest proportion of the 500
Copies, at a loss, to Mr. Arch a
London Bookseller."

LYRICAL BALLADS,

WITH

A FEW OTHER POEMS.

LONDON:
PRINTED FOR J. & A. ARCH, GRACECHURCH-STREET.
1798.

Poems. London: Printed for J. & A. Arch, Gracechurch-Street'. A copy of *this* version is preserved in the extensive Wordsworth Collection held by St John's College Library.

The book neatly illustrates the confusions of its own publication history: a page of advertisements at the back begins 'Published For Joseph Cottle, Bristol, Mr. T. Longman, and Messrs. Lee and Hurst, Paternoster-Row, London', with no mention of Arch at all. It also illustrates how quickly Wordsworth and Coleridge's interests changed over the year in which *Lyrical Ballads* was assembled. The copies circulated under Cottle's name contained a poem by Coleridge titled 'Lewti; or, The Circassian Love Chant', an exotic ballad of unrequited love based on a schoolboy composition of Wordsworth's. In Arch's *Lyrical Ballads*, 'Lewti' was replaced by the blank verse piece 'The Nightingale, A Conversational Poem', in which Coleridge himself seems to communicate reflections on nature to his friends. This shift from ballad to blank verse, and from narrative to meditation, mirrors that which occurred as the whole collection developed. *Lyrical Ballads* was instigated by Coleridge's 'Rime of the Ancient Mariner', a supernatural tale indebted to the eighteenth-century vogue for old ballads, but the last work composed for it was 'Lines Written a Few Miles above Tintern Abbey', a blank verse poem in which Wordsworth seems to communicate thoughts of his own.

Ruth Abbott

....

Opposite: Besides books and manuscripts, the Wordsworth Collection contains artefacts such as Wordsworth's breakfast set and this delightful preliminary drawing by Henry William Pickersgill for his oil painting of the poet commissioned by the College. Above: Title page, and a comment on the initial unpopularity and neglect of Lyrical Ballads.

Mapping a Nation

The Ordnance Survey index,
early nineteenth century

Illustrated here is the Ordnance Survey's first map index, printed from copper on a sheet of handmade paper. Surrounded by a single-line border marked off by ticks at one-degree intervals is a map of southern England, colour-washed by county. Thirty-two numbered quadrilaterals overlay the map, rectangular in the west and the east though on different meridians, representing the earliest sheets to be published in what at the time was the Ordnance Survey's only map, now known as the Old Series. When completed in 1873 it covered England and Wales in 110 sheets at the inch-to-a-mile scale.

Publication of the Old Series had commenced in 1805 with the four sheets covering the county of Essex, followed in 1809 by the eight Devon sheets. The remaining twenty sheets present here appeared between 1810 and 1819. But the war against Napoleon prevented the map being made public and it was not until 1816 that these new sheets became generally available. With the peace evolved a new sales policy. There is evidence of this in advertisements; in the publication of this, the Ordnance Survey's first printed index; and in the practice of packaging and selling the inch-to-a-mile map in groups of flat sheets bound inside buff paper wrappers. These have title panels announcing 'Ordnance Survey of Great Britain. Part the 1st [etc.]', followed by details of the counties present on the sheets within. There would be nine such parts: the sheets comprising the first eight constitute this state of the index. All nine parts (the last covered Pembrokeshire and Lundy, published 1818–20) are present in St John's College Library in this atlas format. These atlases were discontinued in the mid-1820s following decisions to price and sell sheets individually. The College, or the original owner of the College's collection, continued purchasing the map until the Machynlleth, Dunwich and Eye sheets had been published in 1837; to that date this may well be the finest 'as published' set still in existence.

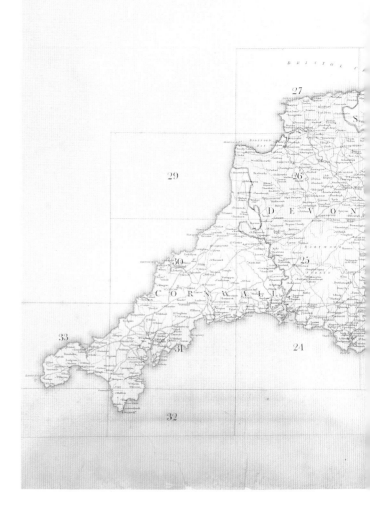

This index is at the ten-mile scale, and is a topographic map showing place-names, roads (later there would additionally be railways), crosses marking parish churches, county boundaries, and also several significant details irrelevant to its function as an index. These include military and navigational sites such as Martello towers at Pevensey, barracks at Hythe, the prison on Dartmoor, sea marks near Walton-le-Soken and Brading, the Longships Lighthouse, and the breakwater at Plymouth. The care with which the estates of the gentry have been mapped suggests a

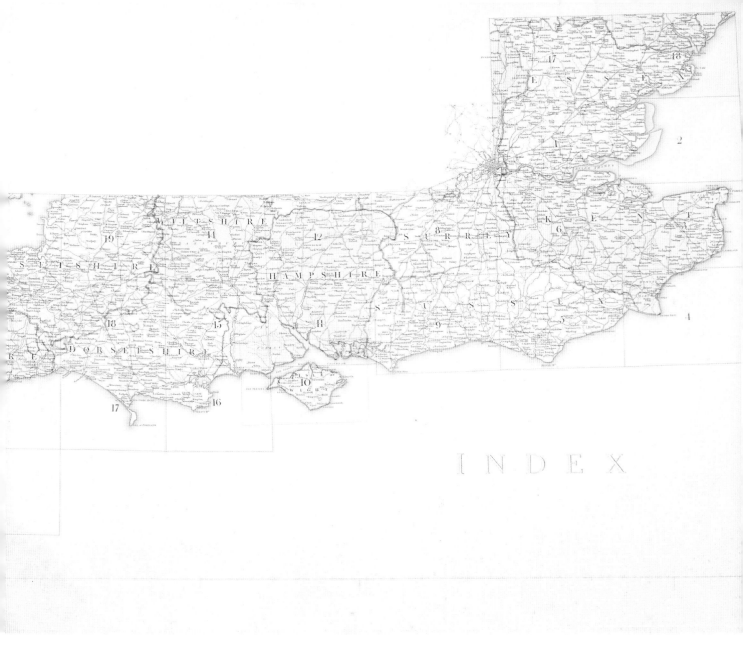

INDEX

recognition of the principal market anticipated for the inch-to-the-mile map, and indeed these estates would later be enhanced on the index by being named, the parkland stippled and enclosed in delicate paling boundaries. Such palings are already present here around Richmond Park on the partly surveyed West London sheet, and the two estates on the Isle of Wight where parkland has also been stippled.

Two less complete states of the index are recorded, one copy annotated 'Unfinished – to be exchanged when completed'. Even on the St John's copy the mapping is not quite finished: still to come are the Eddystone Lighthouse, the completion of a few roads in Kent and Devon, and the ornamentation of uncultivated areas such as the New Forest and Romney Marsh. Over the next seventy years, in parallel with the inch-to-the-mile maps, the index would be extended north on three sheets to cover the whole of England and Wales, and then Scotland.

Roger Hellyer

Student Mischief?

Percy Shelley, *The Necessity of Atheism*, 1811. St John's College Aa.6.15

Percy Shelley was already a published poet when he went up to Oxford in 1810, having put out a volume of *Original Poetry by Victor and Cazire* with his sister Elizabeth earlier that year. He was already the subject of some controversy too: *Victor and Cazire* was withdrawn hurriedly on the discovery that one of the poems had been plagiarised from Matthew 'Monk' Lewis, a deception which Shelley rather ungallantly blamed on his sister.

An Oxford publication co-written with his friend and fellow-undergraduate at University College, Thomas Jefferson Hogg, created an even greater scandal. The teenage Shelley had by this point developed a scepticism 'thro' deficiency of proof' towards the teachings of the Christian Church, and his agnosticism, or 'atheism' as he himself termed it, found expression in this short pamphlet, *The Necessity of Atheism*, published anonymously at Worthing in 1811.

Having published the work, Shelley was not inclined to let it lie neglected. Copies were sent, under a variety of assumed names, to every Oxford college. Predictably, the university authorities took a dim view of what they saw as disrespectful, heretical juvenilia. The Oxford publisher John Munday had refused to print the work, so Shelley and Hogg mischievously placed copies in the window of Munday's shop. When found, these were burned forthwith in the back kitchen. Shelley and Hogg refused to deny authorship and were both sent down by their staunchly Anglican College.

Copies appear to have gone to the heads of some Cambridge colleges too. Ironically, the copy received in St John's was bound up by the then Master James Wood – presumably unread – with a collection of 'Theological Tracts', was bequeathed as such to the College Library in 1839, and was only revealed in its true colours decades later. While there is no great theological power in the argument, and while authorities are divided on whether this is about atheism or agnosticism, the little pamphlet sets out on a robust quest for 'truth', since 'truth has always been found to promote the best interests of mankind'. It makes elegant and very assured reading. Shelley's tone is confirmed by a particularly sweeping and confident concluding sentence: 'Every reflecting mind must allow that there is no proof of the existence of a Deity. Q.E.D.'

Mark Nicholls

Advertisement.

—◆—

As a love of truth is the only motive which actuates the Author of this little tract, he earnestly entreats that those of his readers who may discover any deficiency in his reasoning, or may be in posession of proofs which his mind could never obtain, would offer them, together with their objections to the Public, as briefly, as methodically, as plainly as he has taken the liberty of doing. Thro' deficiency of proof.

AN ATHEIST.

Unfinished Masterpieces

Samuel Taylor Coleridge, *Christabel; Kubla Khan, a Vision; The Pains of Sleep*, 1816.
St John's College 15.53.25

Samuel Taylor Coleridge's fascinating poem 'Christabel' remains something of a mystery. This is partly because it was never finished: Coleridge added successive sections every year between 1798 and 1801, and presented it with 'three parts yet to come' when it finally came out in 1816. But it is also hard to tell what happens even in what we have.

Events unfold as follows: a lady called Christabel leaves her castle at night to pray; she meets another lady called Geraldine and takes her home; Geraldine exhibits troubling behaviour and reveals something shocking and indescribable on her body as she undresses in Christabel's bedroom, casting a spell binding Christabel to silence; the next morning, Christabel's father welcomes Geraldine, but Christabel herself starts exhibiting troubling behaviour, alienating all but the castle bard by asking Geraldine to leave. There it breaks off. Is Geraldine a witch, or a cursed innocent? Is Christabel implicated, or cursed herself? And what was under Geraldine's clothes?

Perhaps there is not supposed to be an answer: Coleridge's friend Charles Lamb thought the poem was intentionally fragmentary, and declared himself 'very angry with Coleridge, when I first heard that he had written a second canto, and that he intended to finish it'. But after its publication in a pamphlet alongside 'Kubla Khan, a Vision' and 'The Pains of Sleep', Coleridge insisted that he had always had an explanation planned. This copy of the pamphlet, once belonging to his son Derwent but now preserved in the Library, suggests why. 'Christabel' influenced Coleridge's contemporaries long before publication; handwritten copies circulated, and Wordsworth, Byron and Walter Scott all declared themselves indebted to it. But on publication, the poem was attacked. Rumours spread that

CHRISTABEL.   7

She folded her arms beneath her cloak,

And stole to the other side of the oak.

  What sees she there?

There she sees a damsel bright,

Drest in a silken robe of white,

~~Her neck, her ~~

~~And the jewels disorder'd in her hair.~~

I guess, 'twas frightful there to see

A lady so richly clad as she—

Beautiful exceedingly!

Mary mother, save me now!

(Said Christabel,) And who art thou?

The lady strange made answer meet,

And her voice was faint and sweet :—

Have pity on my sore distress,

I scarce can speak for weariness.

it was obscene – that Geraldine was secretly a man. So Coleridge defended himself by insisting till his death that 'I always had the whole plan entire from beginning to end in my mind' – and one of the places where he did so is in the St John's copy. On the flyleaf, in 1819, Coleridge wrote: 'I still cherish the hope of finishing this poem, and if by any means I can command two months' actual leisure at the sea side, I hope to finish it in the course of the present year. Enough at present to assure you, that Geraldine is *not* a Witch, in any proper sense of that word – That she is a man in disguise, is a wicked rumour sent abroad.' He then added handwritten corrections responding to critics' accusations, including a couplet about Geraldine's 'Womanhood': where one reviewer had detected sexual innuendo in the word 'leaps', for example, Coleridge crossed it out and wrote 'sprang' above as a replacement.

Perhaps this is unsurprising in a copy belonging to his son! But it also suggests that Coleridge was being defensive: that Lamb was right, and that what mattered in 'Christabel' as first conceived was not Geraldine's identity, but the fact that her identity was impossible to ascertain.

Ruth Abbott

Far left: *Coleridge's note expressing hopes of finishing his poem.*

Left: *Annotations by the author against the printed text of 'Christabel', p. 7.*

Who Discovered Neptune?

The Neptune Notebook of John Couch Adams, 1840s. From St John's College MS W.16

John Couch Adams FRS (1819–92) was a self-taught mathematician who was admitted to St John's in 1839. In 1843 he won first place in the Smith's Prize examination, the forerunner of Part III of the Mathematical Tripos. For this major achievement the College awarded him a Fellowship, held until 1852, when he reached the limit of tenure under the statutes.

His enduring claim to fame arises when, using only mathematics, he correctly predicted the position of the planet Neptune as a means of accounting for the irregularities in the orbit of Uranus, discovered by William Herschel in 1781. When Adams died his wife Eliza preserved his loose pages of notes, and passed them to the College at the end of the nineteenth century. In 1901 the present volume was organised

into the correct chronological sequence by Professor R. A. Sampson, a mathematician who graduated from St John's in 1888, and who had been a student of Adams. The notebook is a full record of Adams's attack on the problem, and the only detailed record we have of the laborious steps that led him to a brilliant solution.

The first page in the book is a memorandum that Adams penned in 1841, when he wrote that he intended to work on the perturbations of Uranus 'as soon as possible after taking my degree'. At this point several astronomers had toyed with the notion that an unseen planet beyond Uranus was perturbing the latter's orbit. By the time Adams resolved to settle the matter the conclusion of the professionals was that a single disturbing planet would not suffice. In the

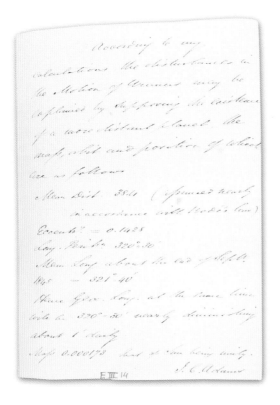

memorandum, Adams decides to solve the intellectual puzzle using just one planet, confident that his investigation would 'probably lead to its discovery'.

The manuscript shows that his first step was to collect all the published observations of Jupiter, Saturn and Uranus since 1781. He used the tables for 1781–1821 assembled by Eugène Bouvard of the Paris Observatory. From 1821 onwards he searched the literature, copying published observations onto slips of paper that he stuffed into his pocket.

By the Long Vacation of 1843 Adams was ready to make his first solution. He assumed that the unseen planet moved in a circular orbit around the Sun at a distance twice that of Uranus. This earliest solution (he made a further five) is the most interesting part of the notebook. It is complete and intelligible, though fiendishly difficult to follow. The handwriting suggests that he worked very fast, racing through fabulous computations without error.

In 1845 he sent his sixth solution for the position of the planet to the Astronomer Royal, George Biddell Airy, who initially took no action. The following year Airy corresponded with Urbain Le Verrier in Paris, who was working on the position of the disturbing planet. Airy then urged the Cambridge Observatory to search for it, but unfortunately they did not possess a star map for the suggested search zone. Meanwhile Le Verrier's prediction reached the Berlin Observatory, which did have a suitable map, allowing Johann Galle to find Neptune on the very first night of the search.

Simon Mitton

....

Far left: Summary of Adams's results in September 1845. Left: Portrait of Adams by Thomas Mogford. Below: Formation of equations for Adams's second hypothesis.

How Undergraduates used to Live

The diary of Francis Hutton, 1846–9. St John's College MS W.33

Until fairly recent times, few contemporary accounts of undergraduate life survive. A rare but notably lively example is the manuscript diary of Francis Hutton, who was up in Cambridge between 1846 and 1849 and who wrote it for a brother then living in New Zealand. Hutton was sociable and frequently served tea, egg flip and wine in his rooms to pipe-smoking undergraduates. He regretted 'the want of female company' on such occasions. That regret will not surprise the modern reader. What might surprise is Hutton's stated reason for it: 'A lot of young spirits together need one or two petticoats to keep them within bounds.' Perhaps he had alcohol intake in mind here, since he records that after one of his parties a friend 'stayed behind – to puke: which feat he performed to his complete satisfaction, in my "Wife", which is the College soubriquet for a "pot de chamber".'

Hutton also took religion very seriously. 'Cambridge is so full of temptations … The only way to guard against them is to be constantly in prayer to our God for help against them.' Work came last in his order of priorities, and he rarely mentions it in his diary except to say that it has been 'put off' once again. He writes that he found the staple diet of classics and mathematics lectures 'excessively stupid and uninteresting'. Accordingly, on the day before examinations began he found himself in a 'terrible funk':

It was now 10.30pm and I had not looked at an Algebra for two years. I rushed down stairs to the man beneath me, and asked him to lend me one – he had no such thing … Off I went over the way to Jones's lodgings, and found him out. However I found an old Algebra – and returned in very good spirits to my rooms, tho' sadly fearful for the morrow. There was no time to lose, so set to work, and read away to the Binomial Theorem by three o'Clock in the morning, when I closed the book, took a pipe, in order to digest what I had read … When I got into bed, I could not sleep … I took morphine – but all was of no avail. I lay awake – and thought what a great ass I had been not to read when I had time … Well, I got out of bed, dreadfully sleepy, at 8 o'C on the Friday, took coffee and started for the Senate House … I felt in a dreadful state of nervousness when I took my seat in the Senate, and it increased to an awful degree when I got the paper, for sure I was a dead plank – my head fell on my hand and I gave way to despair and fell into a sound sleep. Presently I felt someone tapping me; so I looked up, and saw the Director standing over me. 'You have been thinking a long time' he said, 'so pray set to work, or I fear the consequences for you.' I thanked him for his kindness and told him I did not feel very well, which was the fact. However, the sleep had refreshed me, and I began to work.

The examiners were merciful and to his great relief Francis scraped a second class. As a parting shot he wrote, 'Thank God, my University troubles are over, and I am about to commence life in earnest.'

Boyd Hilton

Franchester Ch

Saturday. I have been quite unable to write this week regularly as I
could wish, as I have been much engaged in seeking for rooms. Incumbents
will likely soon be here, and I would like to get a respectable place
amongst the old ones, which in all probability will not be very difficult. I send a sketch of Franchester Church above, from
memory. It is something like — [VRIGHT] I drank tea with our last
night. Do you remember him — an Irish, he and his brother?
If I knew him I shall call on them tonight at any rate. Dr. Browns

Sunday. Nov. 22. Went to All Saints in the morning, and heard a very good
sermon on behalf of the schools, but alas! not having put any money in
my pocket, I was unable to contribute even a mite towards so good and
laudable an object. In the afternoon I went to St Mary's and heard a
splendid sermon from Dr Wordsworth. It was the last of a course of sermons
he was preaching before the University on "The Church" and ably has
he handled this very difficult subject. I shall be well satisfied they
purchased a copy of them should they be printed — which will in all likeli-
hood, be the case. In today's discourse he vigorously repelled the charge
advanced against us by the Romanists, that we were schismatics — Donatists —
and in an impure state — he shewed that they forced us to separate from
them, or rather, rent from them but for their corruptions and anti Scrip-
tural doctrines — and he brought as a parallel the history of the desired reformation under Hezekiah, Isaiah etc. Isaiah, Jeremiah and Ezekiel.
He rebutted the charge of Donatism by shewing that they, by excommun-
icating all those who did not receive her dogmas, and implicitly obey
her commands, laid themselves open to a far more serious and dreadful
charge of Donatism than they were able to bring against us, for our

In the Desert of the Exodus

The 'scrap album' of Edward Henry Palmer, 1859–70. St John's College MS W.15

Edward Henry Palmer (1840–82) matriculated at St John's in 1863, became a Fellow in 1867 and was elected Lord Almoner's Professor of Arabic by the University in 1871. He was an exceptional linguist, expert in Arabic, Persian and Hindustani. His early death was the result of an ambush in the Sinai peninsula, where he had been sent to secure Bedouin support for the British campaign against the Egyptian nationalist leader Arabi Pasha; Palmer had visited Sinai on two previous expeditions with a scholarly historical purpose, and these are described in his *The Desert of the Exodus* (Cambridge, 1872).

His 'scrap album' was bought in 1914 by Sir Robert Scott, then Master of the College, from Palmer's nephew; when offered to the College the Fellows had thought the asking price too high! It was bequeathed by Scott to the College Library in 1933. The earliest dated item in it is a signed drawing of an unidentified church from October 1859, when Palmer was recovering in Cambridge from a serious illness. Several more illustrate the enjoyment of undergraduate friendships at the College which accompanied his devotion to study: he was already publishing work on Oriental literature at this time, while attending to his Classical studies. But most of the 110 drawings, paintings and cuttings relate to the two journeys through Sinai, Palestine and Syria in 1868–70. The first was made as a member of the British Ordnance Survey expedition to western and southern Sinai, which needed Palmer's linguistic expertise to copy inscriptions and record place-names accurately. Items in the album from this journey mostly show scenes in the vicinity of the traditional site of Mount Sinai, above St Catherine's Monastery, or individuals whom Palmer met, such as 'Mûsa my music teacher'.

On his second journey Palmer travelled with Charles Tyrwhitt Drake to explore the region between Mount Sinai and Palestine known as Badiet et-Tih, 'the desert of the wandering', and southern Transjordan. A central aim was to clarify aspects of the route taken by the Israelites in the Exodus from Egypt. The album contains over sixty scenes from this journey, a few drawn by Drake but most, apparently, by Palmer himself. Although only some of them are arranged in chronological order, their sequence can be reconstructed with the help of the detailed narrative in *The Desert of the Exodus*. There are views of mountains, hills, ravines, wells, ancient buildings and caves, including some of Petra and the journey's continuation to Jerusalem and beyond. They provide an invaluable visual supplement to the smaller number of illustrations included in Palmer's book. In some cases they even fill gaps in written accounts of the journey, published and unpublished, such as visits to Mount Carmel and Tiberias. One painting has a special interest because of modern archaeological discoveries at the site now known as Kuntillet 'Ajrûd. Dozens of inscriptions from the time of the Israelite monarchy were found there in the 1970s, including some that mention 'Yahweh and his asherah', and these have had a dramatic impact on studies of the Old Testament. Palmer and Drake themselves dug into the ruins, and the upper painting opposite shows a half-exposed jar very like those on which many of the inscriptions were written.

Graham Davies

....

Opposite: Kuntillet 'Ajrûd; 'Tiberias and the Lake of Gennazereth'. Overleaf: Camel, Sinai; In Wadi Wutâh; 'Ain Hudhera, Sinai; From Jebel 'Aráif, et Tih.

Contellet Saraiyeh
The Tih.

Tiberias & the Lake of Gennazareth

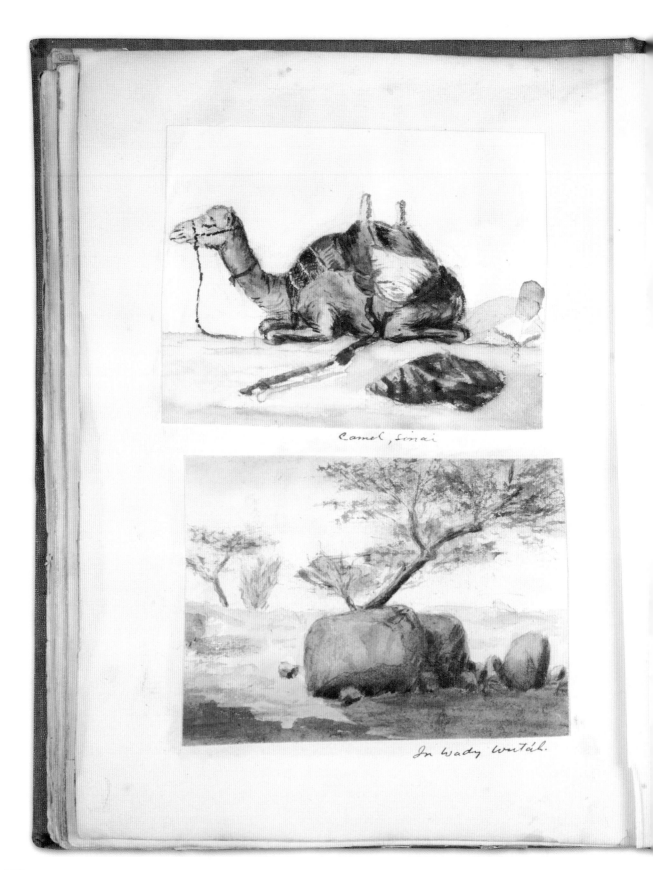

Camel, Sinai

In Wady Wutáh.

Ain Hudhera, Sinai

From Jebel 'Arâif, et Bh

A Victorian Photographer Takes to the Road

The Samuel Butler Collection, late nineteenth century

The Victorian polymath Samuel Butler (1835–1902) is predominantly remembered for his novels, *Erewhon* and *The Way of All Flesh*, but he was also an accomplished artist and a pioneering photographer. His substantial legacy is well represented in the Library's collection, which includes more than 1700 black-and-white prints produced by Butler and almost the same number of his original glass plate negatives, mostly dating from the period 1888–99.

Having trained at art school in London during the 1860s and 1870s and failed to achieve the recognition that he desired, Butler turned his attention to the relatively new medium of photography, which unlike painting was free from expectations and conventions. This freedom, coupled with the ability to capture images almost at the same speed as thoughts, suited Butler perfectly. As he documented in his *Notebooks*: 'One's thoughts fly so fast that one must shoot them; it is

no use trying to put salt on their tails.' He referred to his photographs as 'snap-shots', an enduring term that neatly sums up his informal attitude to the camera and its purpose.

During the 1880s collodion 'wet plates' were replaced by 'dry plate' negatives – thin pieces of glass pre-prepared with a light-sensitive emulsion – an innovation which enabled photographers for the first time to work freely outdoors and to travel with their negatives before developing them. This heralded the rise of amateur photography. Like many others, Butler promptly acquired the latest affordable, mass-produced equipment, which he carried with him on his frequent expeditions to Europe. The range of his subjects, the skill of his compositions and the volume of his output distinguish Butler from the majority of amateurs. His recognisable style manifests his unique way of viewing the details of everyday life, which better-known writer-photographers of the period, such as Zola and Strindberg, tended to overlook.

As well as documenting the cities, towns, villages and cultural sites Butler visited, the photographs reveal his deep interests. It was *situations* – not landscapes or architecture or portraits or artefacts, but the live relationships that existed between them – that most frequently caught Butler's eye. His images are some of the earliest in the history of photography to have captured real life as it unfolded, unselfconsciously, in the moment.

In particular, the photographs demonstrate Butler's fascination with people. Many highlight individuals absorbed in their work, engaged in conversations and transactions, or isolated within bustling crowds. People on the margins of society always interested Butler, and some of the more striking images communicate his genuine empathy for his subjects. Empathy and an instinctive sense of comedy also radiate from the numerous depictions of animals, another of Butler's favoured subjects; having made a living as a sheep farmer in the early years of the New Zealand settlements he appreciated the important, complex roles animals often play in the lives of individuals and communities.

Rebecca Watts

*Opposite: Man with Monkey. Varallo. 7 September 1891 (Album 1/50/4; Glass plate negative D89.2); Goat stealing horse's food. Athens. 18 April 1895 (Album 4/15/5; Glass plate negative D77.11). **Above:** Sheep on Boat. Smyrna. 30 April 1895 (Album 4/22/6; Glass plate negative D85.12). **Right:** Women Washing. Trapani. 9 August 1893 (Album 3/18/6; Glass plate negative D19.4); Rue de Rivoli. Paris. 9 June 1892 (Album 2/13/5; Glass plate negative D104.3).*

Grasping the Essence of Things

The Nobel Prize for Physics medal, awarded to Paul Dirac, 1933

On 9 November 1933, Paul Dirac was awarded the Nobel Prize for Physics jointly with Erwin Schrödinger 'for the discovery of new productive forms of atomic theory'. At the same time the prize for the previous year, which had been deferred, was awarded to Werner Heisenberg 'for the creation of quantum mechanics'. Aged thirty-one, Dirac was the youngest theoretical physicist to have received the prize up till then. In his doctoral thesis in 1926 he had reconciled the wave mechanics of Schrödinger and matrix algebra of Heisenberg, two apparently very different approaches to quantum theory, setting them in a more general context and thereby providing the mathematical language for describing quantum phenomena that we still use today.

Dirac's Nobel Prize also recognised what was perhaps his greatest achievement, universally known as the Dirac equation. Universally, that is, except in Dirac's own lectures and writings, in which it was described prosaically as 'the relativistic equation for the electron'. Now, carved on a stone commemorating him, placed there in 1994, it is the only mathematical equation to be found in Westminster Abbey.

The Dirac equation, published in 1928, reconciled quantum theory with the first of the great revolutions of physics in the twentieth century, Einstein's special theory of relativity. Dirac saw that previous approaches to this were unsatisfactory and, characteristically using a radically different approach, he produced an equation describing the quantum mechanical motion of the electron, consistent with relativity but necessarily requiring that it had very definite properties – spin and magnetic moment – which agreed with experiment.

The implications of the equation went further. As Dirac pointed out in 1931, it required the existence of a particle of the opposite charge but the same mass as the electron, the anti-electron or positron, which could annihilate with the electron to produce energy in the form of light (photons).

Above: Portrait of Dirac by Michael Noakes.

This particle was discovered experimentally in 1932. Heisenberg described this prediction of the existence of antimatter as 'the most decisive discovery in connection with the nature of elementary particles … [It] changed our whole outlook on atomic physics completely.'

The first years of Dirac's research career fell in a golden age that he himself did much to create. In later years, ignoring fashion, he continued to produce seminal papers whose influence has grown with the years. On retirement, he and his wife went to live in Florida, often coming back to the College in the summer. On the last such occasion the Master, Harry Hinsley, offered to keep Dirac's gown in the Master's Lodge to await his return, and there it hangs still. Unable to return for the customary dinner on 27 December 1982,

the Feast of St John the Evangelist following his eightieth birthday, when, by custom, the Fellows would drink a toast to him, he wrote to the Master: 'When the Fellows drink my health please give them my regrets that I am not with them … Also tell them that for 59 years the College has been the central point of my life and a home to me.'

Dirac had entered St John's as a graduate student in 1923 and was a Fellow from 1927 until his death in 1984. In line with his wishes, his widow gave his Nobel Prize medal to the College. For some years the certificate that accompanies the medal was mislaid, but once it was found his daughter, Monica, gave it in 2006 to Graham Farmelo, Dirac's biographer, to convey to the College.

Peter Goddard

Corresponding with Everyone

The Cecil Beaton Papers

On a crisp day in December 1979 I paid my first visit to Reddish House in Broadchalke, the Wiltshire home of the photographer and designer Sir Cecil Beaton. The pretext was that I was to write a life of the Duke and Duchess of Kent but, though unsaid, the purpose was that I was to be vetted for the job of writing Sir Cecil's authorised life. We had a long talk in his library before lunch. In the shelves to the right of me was a row of large leather-bound boxes, marked with letters of the alphabet. On this visit the boxes remained closed. They looked enticing.

I was appointed, but two days after my second visit, in January 1980, Sir Cecil died. After a discreet interval I went back to Reddish House to start my work. Then it was my duty to open the boxes and inspect the treasures within. The boxes contained the letters of a lifetime, and a treasure chest of gems they proved to be. Here were letters from his parents, and others dating from early friendships to the present day. Eileen Hose, Beaton's faithful secretary, produced my letter to Sir Cecil and later asked me what I had done with it. She smiled when I said: 'I wrote VICKERS on it and put it in the box marked V.'

In these boxes were many clues to the influences on Beaton. I was amazed by the multi-coloured letters of Stephen Tennant. I asked Eileen what had happened to him. He was still alive and living at Wilsford Manor. I took to driving past his house on my way home, observing a light on in an upper room. In due course (another story) I was allowed into his sheltered domain and he proved one of the best sources on the early life of my subject.

After Reddish House was sold, Eileen pondered the fate of the Beaton papers. She consigned the boxes to my care along with the 145 volumes of diaries and the fifty volumes of press cuttings. From 1980 until after I finished my biography, I had them in my London flat. She and I then put our heads together to consider a final resting place for these fascinating papers. As ordained by Cecil's will, the press-cutting books went to the Victoria and Albert Museum. The literary papers had been bequeathed to Eileen as Cecil's acting literary executor.

She was certain that Cecil would not have wanted his papers to go to an American library. He was a passionate British patriot. So we both agreed that Cambridge would be the best place. That decided, there was really only one possible choice of home.

It would be wrong to suggest that Cecil Beaton held his old College, St John's, in high esteem. In later life he claimed seldom to have entered the precincts of the College, and he left Cambridge without a degree and weighed down by debt. Nevertheless, Eileen and I were delighted when the Library at St John's accepted the papers as a gift. Eileen died in 1987 and I succeeded her as literary executor under the terms of her will. In the last quarter of a century I have worked with successive librarians. The papers are beautifully cared for and they are safe for the perusal of scholars for generations to come.

Hugo Vickers

Opposite: Extracts from Beaton's diary for 1934–5. Above inset: Beaton's full-length costume drawing of Costard, from Love's Labour's Lost.

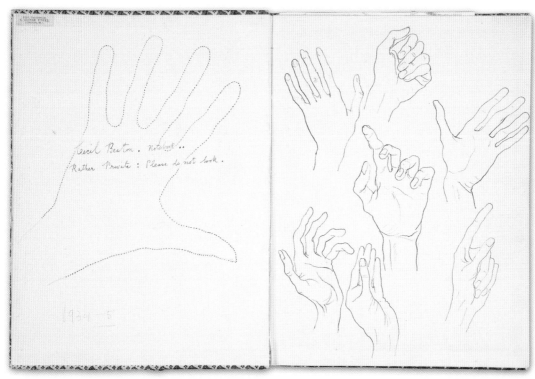

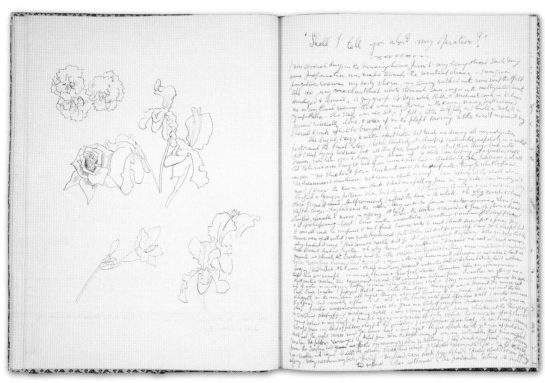

Big Bang!

The Papers of Sir Fred Hoyle

Sir Fred Hoyle FRS (1915–2001) was an astrophysicist, author and media personality. Many of his personal papers, books and artefacts were presented to the College Library by his widow. This extensive and broad collection provides a vivid insight into the life and work of one of the most famous British scientists of the twentieth century.

Hoyle came up to Cambridge in 1933 to read mathematics. He was elected a Fellow of St John's College and appointed

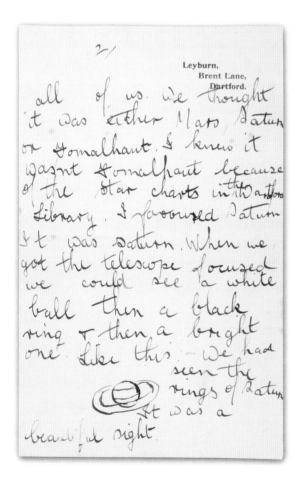

the University's Plumian Professor of Astronomy and Experimental Philosophy. Hoyle came to public prominence in the late 1940s as an advocate of the steady-state theory of the universe. This theory gained little ground among astrophysicists but a series of BBC Radio talks in the early 1950s – delivered in Hoyle's characteristic Yorkshire accent – cemented the public popularity of both the theory and of Hoyle himself.

In his radio talks, Hoyle coined a phrase which quickly came into common parlance. He explained how the counter-theory hypothesised that 'all matter in the universe was created in one big bang at a particular time in the remote past'. Though not used as an out-and-out insult, the phrase 'big bang' was certainly deployed within the context of his obvious disparagement of the theory: 'It is', he said, 'an irrational process that cannot be described in scientific terms.'

Scientifically, Hoyle's outstanding achievement was his contribution to a groundbreaking paper on stellar nucleosynthesis, known among physicists as 'B²FH' after the

which he conceived of the chain reaction for the creation of the elements from oxygen to calcium.

A series of science-fiction novels, many of which were co-authored with his son Geoffrey, provided Hoyle with an outlet for investigating ideas at and beyond the edge of current scientific thinking. They also paint vivid portraits of characters and procedures in the University of Cambridge and at Hoyle's second academic home, the California Institute of Technology, in the 1950s and 1960s. The Hoyle Collection holds manuscripts of many of the novels, together with the author's copies of the published books, translated into every major European language as well as Hebrew and Japanese.

Beyond his professional research, Hoyle turned his enthusiasm towards numerous topics and activities, many of which stirred up controversy in the establishment and beyond. The Hoyle Collection contains evidence for his interest in ice ages, the origins of life and the possibility that viruses exist in interstellar space, economics, the efficacy of badger culls and the purpose of Stonehenge, as well as the (possibly) less controversial topics of hill walking, cricket, tree-leaf shapes, classical music and the mathematics of the football league.

Katherine Birkwood

names of the four authors: Geoffrey Burbidge, Margaret Burbidge, Willy Fowler and Hoyle. Stellar nucleosynthesis is the process by which all chemical elements are made inside stars. (Hoyle once explained to his wife Barbara that 'the iron in your saucepans was made inside the stars'.) Notes preserved in the Hoyle Collection capture the moment at

Opposite: Hoyle's letter to his father in 1930, Hoyle 45.7.1; photograph of Hoyle (right) with Margaret Burbidge, Geoff Burbidge and Willy Fowler. Above left: First edition of Hoyle's science fiction novel The Black Cloud. *Overleaf: Page from Hoyle's notebook, 1946 (Hoyle 85.5) in which he wrote his first calculations and ideas on element synthesis.*

The equilibrium concentrations of He, C, O at 4×10^9 °K when the partial density of He is 10^4 are $10^{27.2}$, $10^{20.2}$, $10^{20.8}$.

Do nuclear reaction rates allow a time scale in which, as the temperature drops, an appreciable proportion of He is converted into C and O? The answer appears to be The reason for this failure is that if the time allowed is kept sufficiently short to prevent O being converted to Ne, then the amount of C built up by triple collisions of He is quite inappreciable.

Table I gives the ~~logarithms~~ logarithms of the probability of a reaction per (heavy) nucleus per taking He density as 10^4

	Temperature	10^8	2×10^8	4×10^8	7×10^8	10^9	1.5×10^9	2×10^9	3×10^9	+
I	$3He^4$	-23.4	-16.5	-12.0	-9.6	-8.4	-7.3	-6.6	-5.9	
	$C^{12} + He^4$	-17.1	-11.0	-6.2	-3.3	-1.6	$+0.1$	$+1.1$	$+2.4$	+
	$O^{16} + He^4$	-23.3	-15.8	-9.8	-6.0	-3.9	-1.9	-0.6	$+1.1$	+

If the probability for the reaction $C^{12} + He^4$ is p, and we choose a time t so that $pt = 1$, then a fraction $\frac{1}{2}$ of the carbon formed by the reaction $3He^4$ will survive. Further, if p' is the corresponding probability for $3He^4$, and $p' \ll p$, then the fraction of helium converted into carbon is about $p't$, $= \frac{p'}{p}$. And this is the roughly maximum fraction that can be converted into C^{12}.

Hence the maximum fraction of He that can be converted into C or O, is given by its logarithms shown in table II

II	C	-6.3	-5.5	-5.8	-6.3	-6.8	-7.4	-7.7	-8.3	$-$
	O	-0.1	-0.7	-2.2	-3.6	-4.5	-5.4	-6.0	-7.0	$-$

Thus an appreciable conversion of He to C seems impossible, and as regards formation of oxygen, the time required at 2×10^8 °K ~~to~~ is of the order of 10^{16} sec, which may be ~~too~~ ~~rather~~ long compared to the rate of contraction of a nova.

Furthermore, the density may be expected to drop as $\rho \propto T^3$. Since the reaction $3He^4$ involves ρ^2, whereas the other reactions involve only ρ', the logarithms in table II would be changed to

III	C		-9.4	-8.3	-8.6	-8.6	-8.7	-8.6	-8.7	$-$
	O	-4.9	-4.6	-5.2	-5.9	-6.3	-6.7	-6.9	-7.4	$-$

Thus the prospects of obtaining C and O by this method seem hopeless.

If we took other values of E_0 or $\sigma(E_0)$, we should obtain other limiting values of n_p. The present value seems reasonable. We have similar requirement on the numbers of α particles

$$n_\alpha \gtrsim \left(\frac{k_T}{E_0}\right)^{\frac{1}{2}} e^{E_0/kT} \Big/ v_\alpha \, \sigma(E_0)$$

Since the number of α particles is always considerably greater than the number of protons in critical cases it seems probable that the protons represent the critical case for freezing. (Note we assume all three particles protons, neutrons, α particles are necessary to give the required chain). For the neutron reactions we have no penetration of a potential barrier and we can write

$$n_N \gtrsim \frac{1}{v_N \sigma(} \quad \sim \frac{1}{3.10^9 \, \sigma} \quad \sim \frac{3.10^{-10}}{\sigma}$$

Since $n_N \gtrsim n_p$ there is no condition n_N for $\sigma > 10^{-31}$.

Example of a chain

$O^{16} + He^4 \rightarrow F^{19} + H^1$

$F^{19} + H^1 \rightarrow Ne^{20} + h\nu$

$Ne^{20} + He^4 \rightarrow Na^{23} + H^1$

$Na^{23} + H^1 \rightarrow Mg^{24} + h\nu$

$Mg^{24} + He^4 \rightarrow Al^{27} + H^1$

$Al^{27} + H^2 \rightarrow Si^{28} + n$

$Si^{28} + He^4 \rightarrow P^{31} + H^1$

$P^{31} + He^4 \rightarrow S^{34} + H^1$

$S^{34} + He^4 \rightarrow Cl^{37} + H_1$

$Cl^{37} + He^4 \rightarrow A^{40} + H_1$

$A^{40} + He^4 \rightarrow Ca^{45} + n$

Index

The Library Treasures of St John's College, Cambridge

2014 © St John's College, Cambridge and
Third Millennium Publishing Limited

First published in 2014 by Third Millennium Publishing Limited,
a subsidiary of Third Millennium Information Limited.

2–5 Benjamin Street
London EC1M 5QL
United Kingdom

www.tmiltd.com

ISBN: 978 1 906507 98 5

British Library Cataloguing in Publication Data
A CIP catalogue record for this book is available from the British Library.

Design	Susan Pugsley
Principal Photographer	Carl Impey (C I Photography)
Production	Debbie Wayment
Reprographics	Studio Fasoli, Verona, Italy
Printing	1010 International Limited, China